Letters Apart

Paintings by Liat Yossifor

Poems by Ed Schad

Letters Apart: Poetry and Painting in the Time of COVID

I had never really given much thought to the air until March 2020. In Los Angeles, the COVID-19 lockdown officially started on the 18th and I was one of many people who had little idea what was coming. What had been a rumor of a virus from Wuhan, China eventually not only came onto my doorstep, but also served to shut the door itself. I was behind it with a ten pound bag of brown rice, a grip of homemade masks, and enough uncertainity to fill evey inch of my house. Outside of the door, the lawn, the street, the neighborhood looked the same, only empty of people (at this point, even going outdoors was discouraged). However, the air was different. I stared at the silence and the totality of it hovering full of fog in the morning and pollen in the afternoon. I distrusted it. The air became a character, a sinister presence.

About two weeks into lockdown, I wanted to see what Liat Yossifor was working on. I had one of her paintings, The Dancer from 2012, and over the years, I have watched it in various shifts of light and weather and circumstance. The small grey work — with the looks of a perpetually wet surface in the process of being mixed into various shades of white and blue — has proved quite the shape-shifter over those eight years, sometimes full of figures dashing to and fro across the panel, sometimes merging into a single face. My best moments with the painting are when I am doing something else, not looking at it at all, and suddenly, there it is, its frenzy of soft brushstrokes snapping into views that will be gone the next day. What Liat works on, as I thought, had something to do with how the air firms up, then melts.

When Liat sent me her new paintings — a selection eventually consolidated into an exhibition at Patron Gallery in Chicago — I wanted to write poems about them and did so. The process was fun. I would stare at them and write down what I saw. I would come back later and stare at them again and the image would move onto something else. I would try and connect my previous notes with my new notes to see if they started to take on music. Anything rhetorical seemed wrong. Liat's paintings do not take firm positions in terms of form; they do not assert an image or a story that demands primacy. Instead, I had to follow the motion of Liat's paint — which she works over and over until it is dry and no longer able to move — as it conjured unusual events of language through a friction of her progression of imagery and my personal memories. If there was a bird, I had to keep the bird in the mind and try to merge it or reconcile it with seeing a chair, a patch of grass, a building, a box, or a bowl of marbles.

I was shy to ask Liat if we could explore her paintings through poetry, though I had already done so in private. However, I was delighted when she not only allowed me to write on her works but started sending images of them to me as they were made during the lockdown. They were letters of a sort and I received them as such, writing a letter back to Liat in verse. At times, the paintings resisted and I would struggle for weeks on them. At other times, I would open the jpeg file and tumble right into a glut of words. Often, the paintings suggested phrases that set the stage for the poem — "A bee in his brain, the bullet," or "Up with confidence, the elders," or "honey pump, glory pump." At other moments, they seemed to tell short stories or even, despite my better judgement, have a rhetorical armature.

What follows in this volume is a partial record of Liat and my communications during lockdown and afterward. Inside of them, I see so many of the events that defined this time for me, both existentially and historically. In the poems, I remember the death of my grandmother, a mass shooting in the San Fernando Valley, a trip to Zion National Park, and several road trips to Texas. I think of the murder of George Floyd, the frenzy and horror of January 6th, and the books that I revisited after decades, all carrying moments that linked to Liat's paintings. Still other poems, it must be said, leave me with the thought of, "What could I have possibly seen here, what could I have possibly been thinking?" I admit to living for moments such as this, where I do not recognize myself in the poem at all.

Mercifully, the specifics of these items are buried and transformed by Liat's pigment and her lines, her handling of the flux and finesse of life. Therefore, they remain buried in my poems as well. Through this project, I was happy that we could share the anxieties of COVID together. Simply put, none of us knew what was happening or what the air would bring, and Liat was a proper guide for me through these matters. Her paintings never stay the same. They have equal capacity for light as darkness. One day, they made me think of Max Beckmann sitting moody on a beach in a fur coat. The next, they made me think of wanting to dramatically squeeze a block of butter. They suggest the weather of life, how crazy it can get, how suffocating it can be, how rich the interaction of the two can become.

A crystal ball on a clean round table,
A pear, at times, a globe, a globe then a fishbowl,
A fishbowl back to a pear, then a bowl of pears,
A dish of apples, a skull, a half jug of wine,
The spout of which, a swan, then guitar neck.
Through the coffee hour and into the night,
A crystal ball on a clean round table.

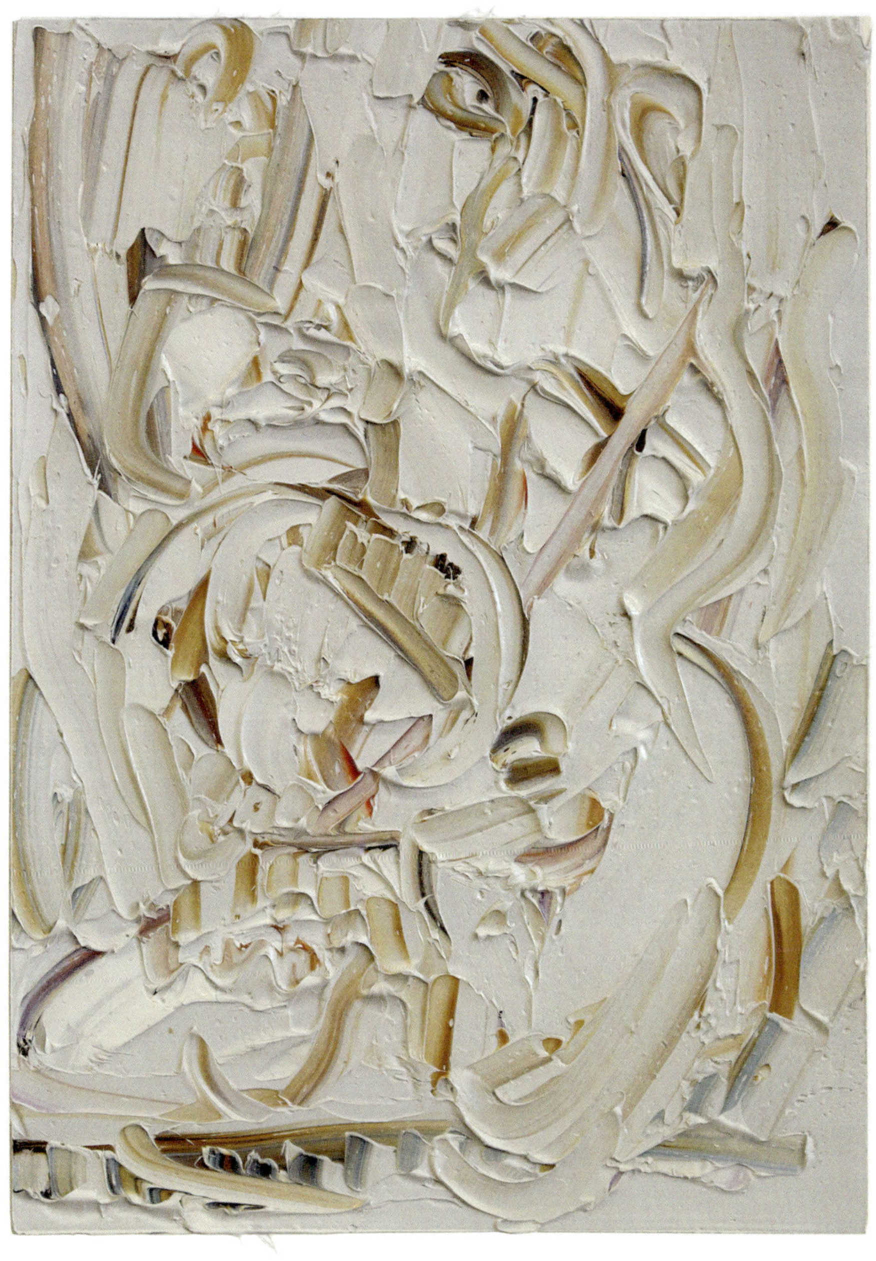

I imagine a horse head
Becoming a saxophone.
Flared nostril tone holes
Take tired farmhands
To an elegant sunset song.

The image cannot last,
I feel my tack and harness,
My legs no longer pull,
My muzzled mouth gasps
Out sweat-exhausted air.

A horn does play, but for itself,
Out there alone, not a function
Of anything I am or could be.

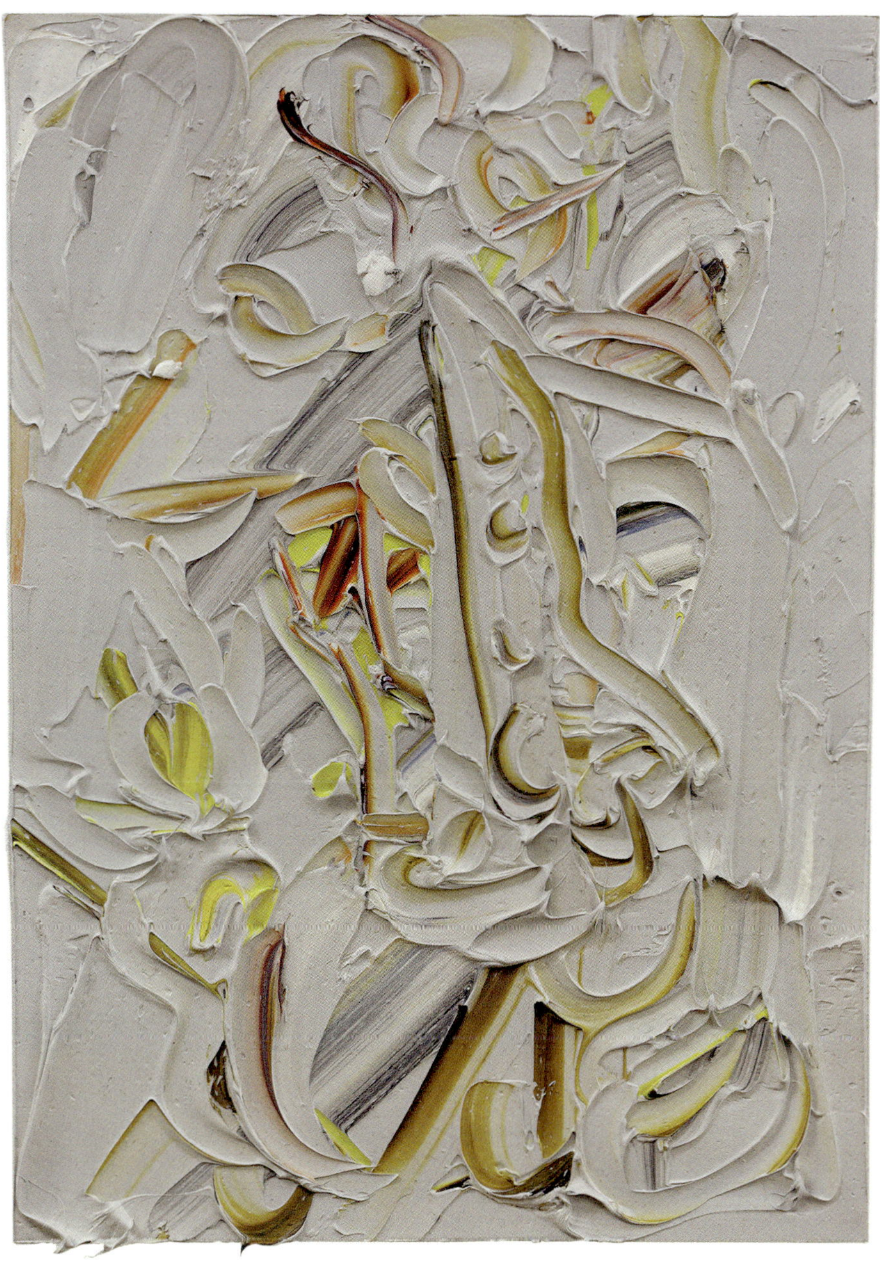

Dutch portraits with decapitating "ruffs,"
Pleated fans and pillows of lace,
Ringing proper ladies and industrious men:
Rembrandt's collar flares, first brash, then ruined.

Ten yards for a single neck, wheels of fine linen,
Boasts atop the simple suits of society.
The stitched folds, virtue under careful wraps,
Enough for warehouses of starch, multi-masted

Holds of fabric brought across channels,
And shamefully open and entitled seas.
Is it wrong to hear the ruff's echo, the millstone
Diver, in the steel elephant trunk of Max Ernst?

In Beckmann's tuxedo as it tightens around his pipe,
In Frida's choker of roots and blood pressured veins,
In the fuel and smoke of Duchamp's chocolate grinder,
Turning, greased and capable, under broken glass?

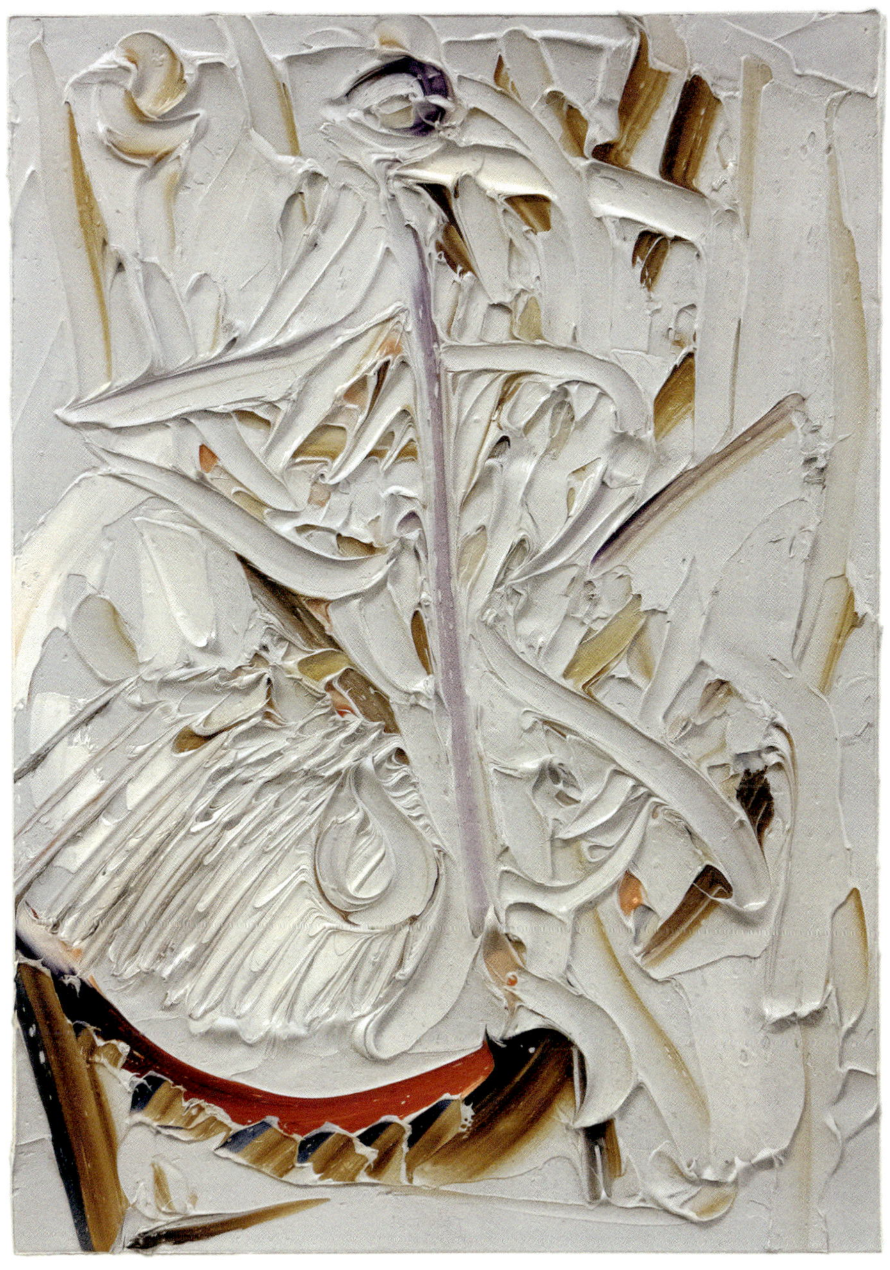

Stones dropped to the river
By course of rope and roller:
Muscles taut, sweat, twisted
squalor under the season's sun.

Boys wet the ropes, tamed
The heat and the friction of power,
Learning lessons of weight and pressure,
Learning details of slack and submission,

Boys at their task, the first
In a chain to kill the wildness
In their hearts, that hot energy
Still living as the stones move.

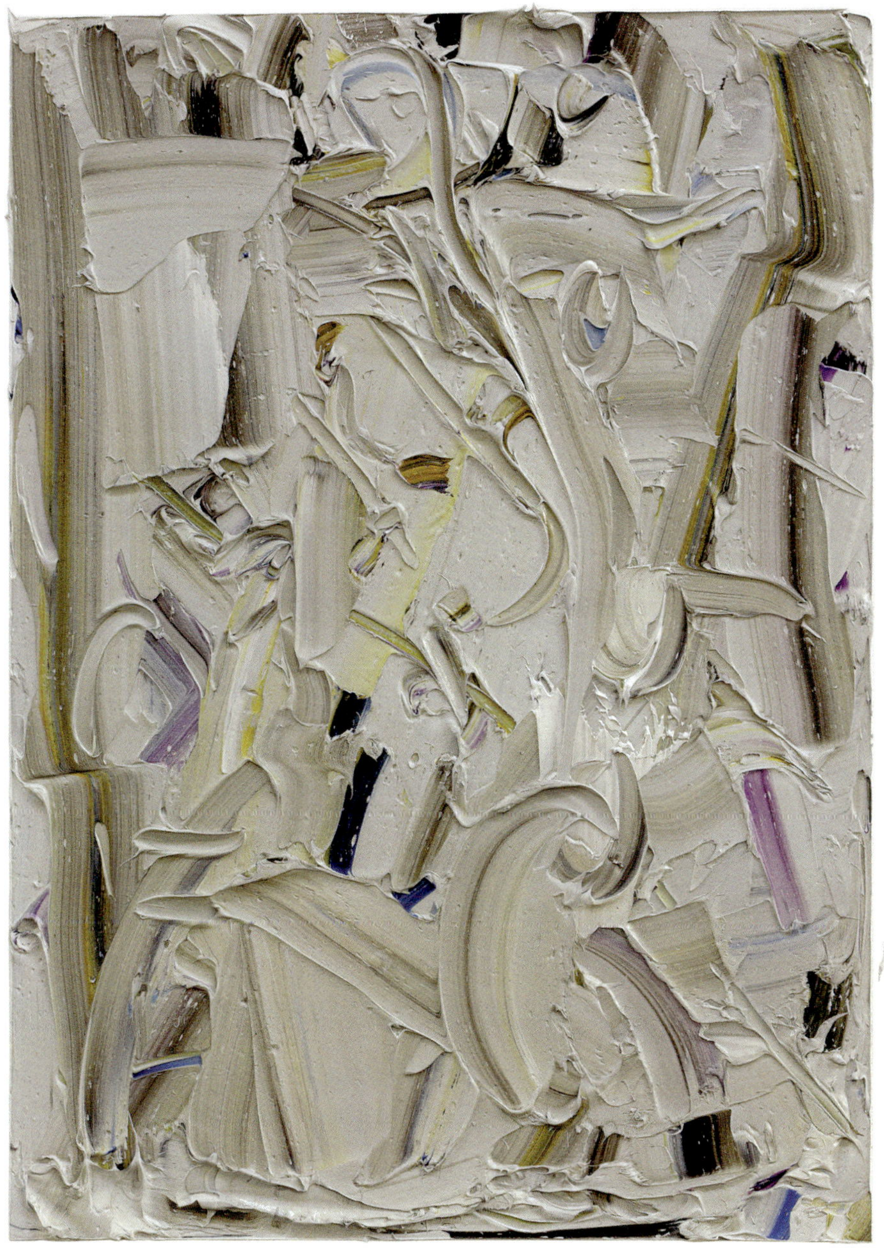

Two hearts, one on a motorcycle,
                    another in a carriage,
Journey through different eras, to their loves.

So goes an equation I read once:
The organ's weight varies by velocity,
And pumps ceaselessly through time.

Yet, these hearts are also tranquil green ponds,
On which algae suspends and fallen leaves float,
Into which single round pebbles are thrown.

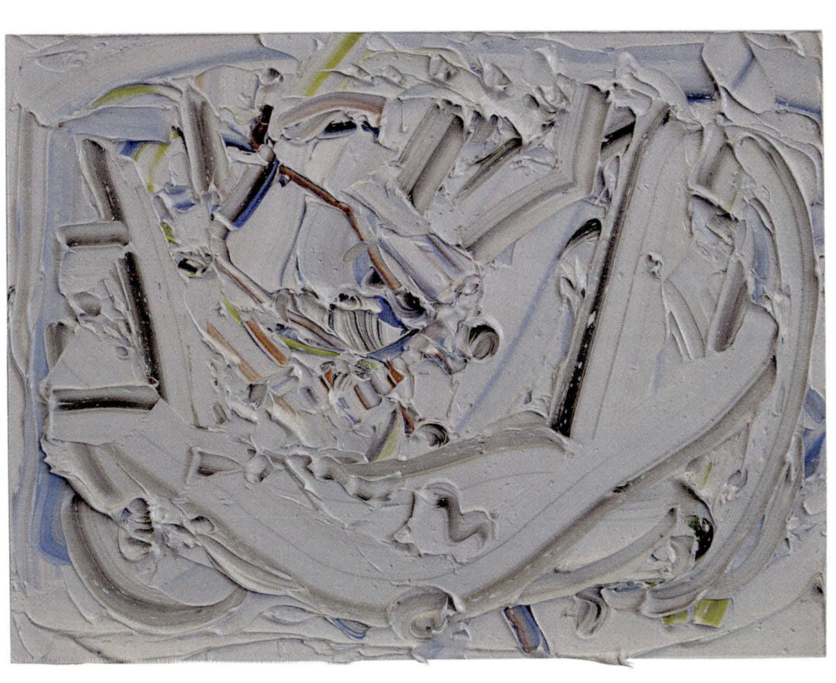

We spun around our table in soft rituals,
Two moons in orbit around a fertile sphere,
Rotating waves of cereal and seasons of fruit.
Tides of blueberry pancakes and curds
Ebbed out into a Sunday of butter and toast.

On our elliptic path, with directional force,
We balanced on a string, all momentum,
Elegant and sweet, hovering sideways
Momentarily away from a world, which
Would chime in soon with its urgent bell.

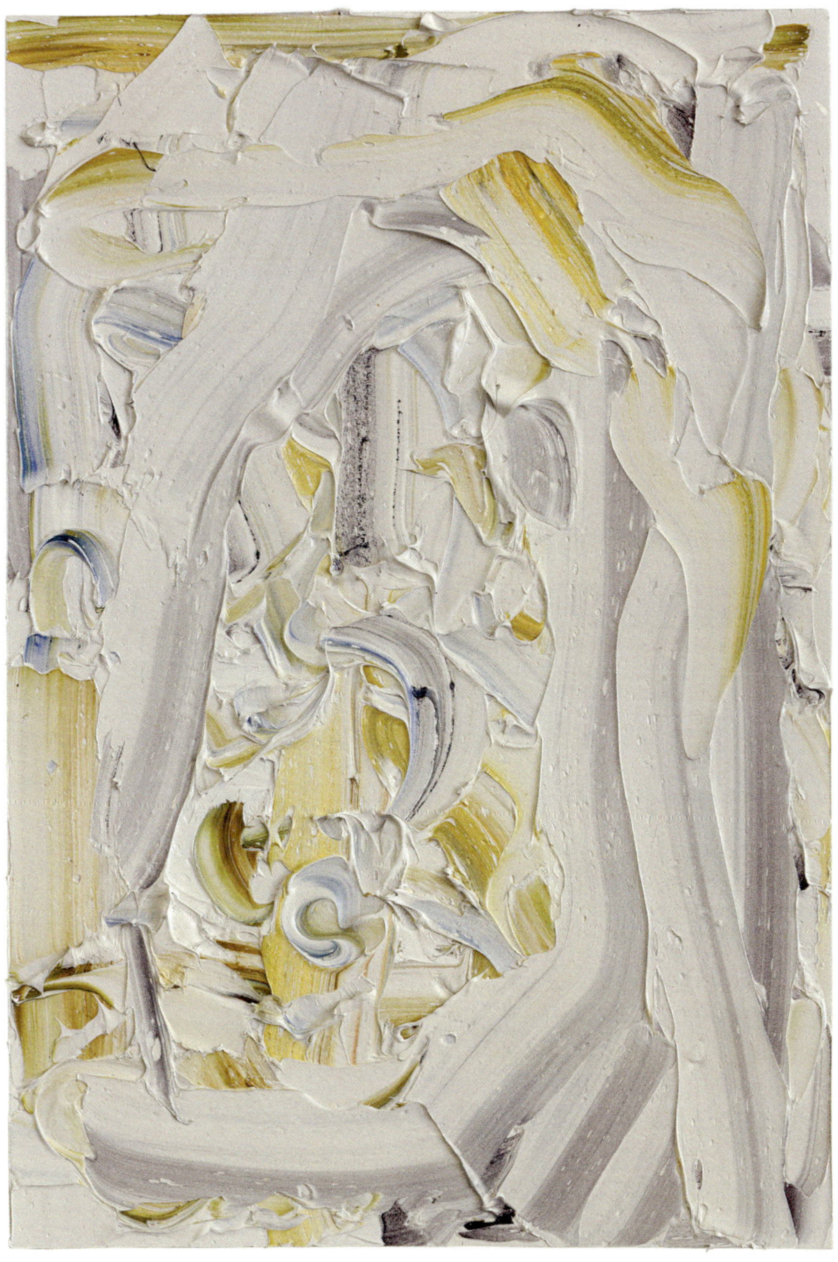

The rivers,
in me and through me,
without logic,
eddied out:

Red choke
Rattlesnake sand

L.A. concrete
Graffiti sea

Brazos piss tube
Beer sink

Colorado lifeblood
Kill switch

Chicago green tide
Catholic spring

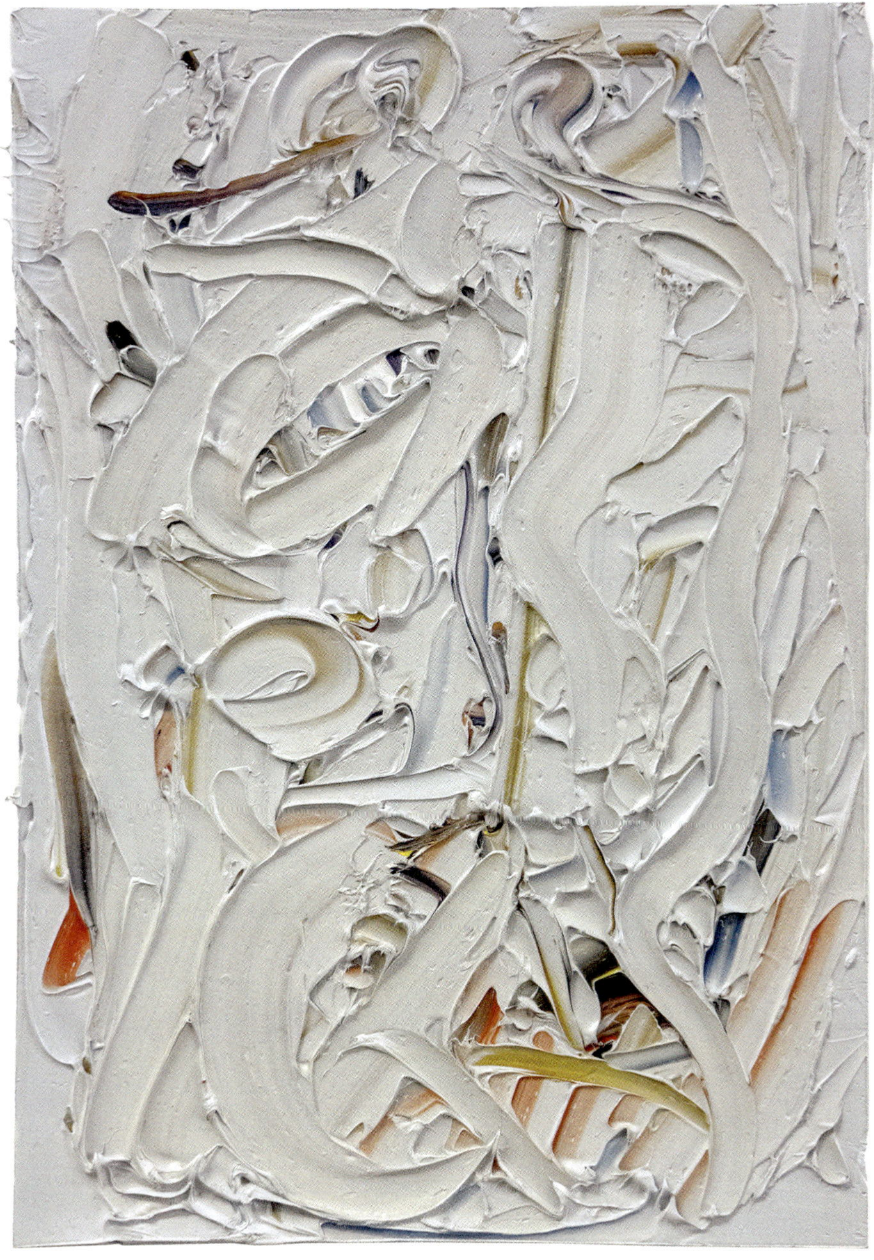

An azure horizon rose to meet the sun, magnanimous,
Bestowing the gift of a breeze and gentle purple light
Onto a beach of morning sand as a couple shared a smile.

I felt them casting their grace my way, as I sat there,
Legs up and eyes out, a man in summer wearing fur,
Inside my fortress, screaming out curses into the air.

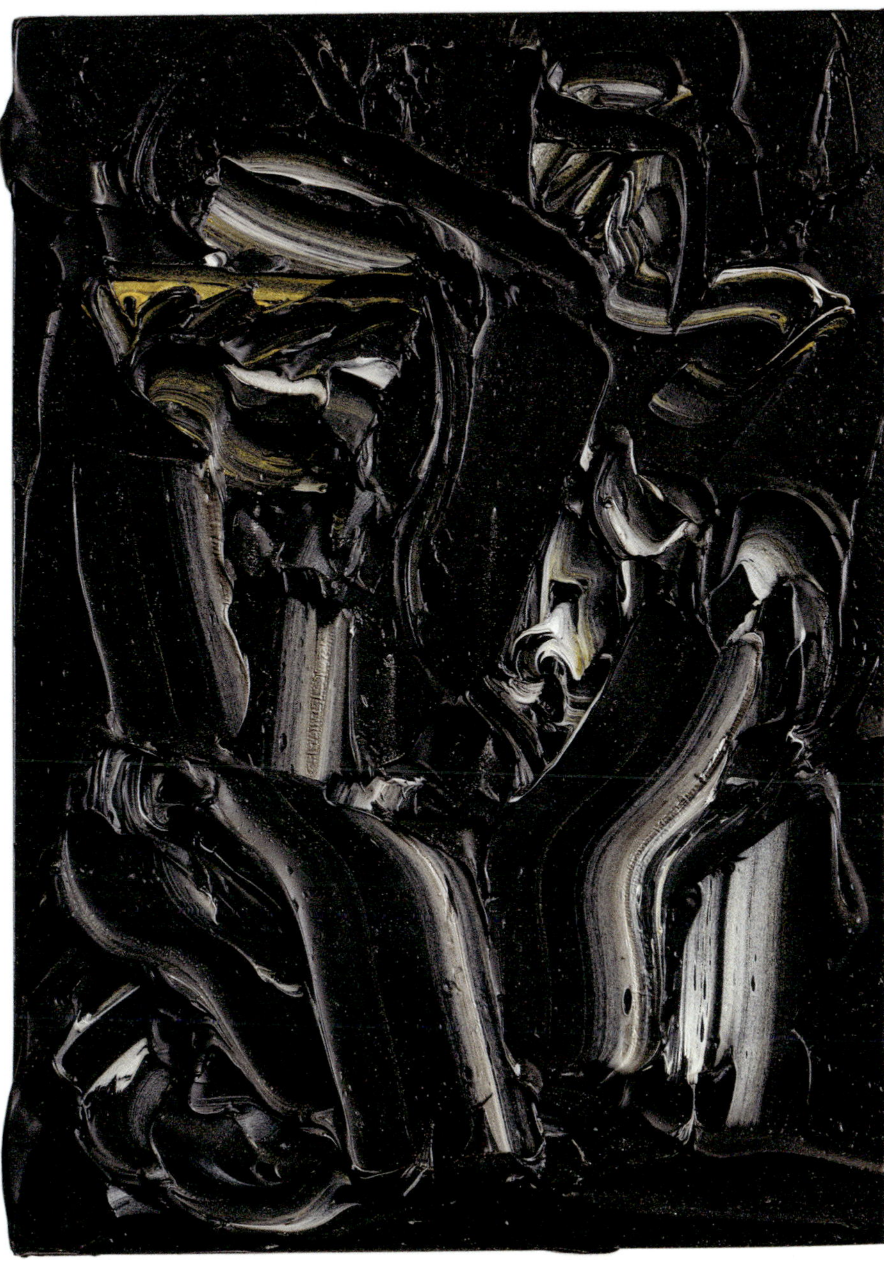

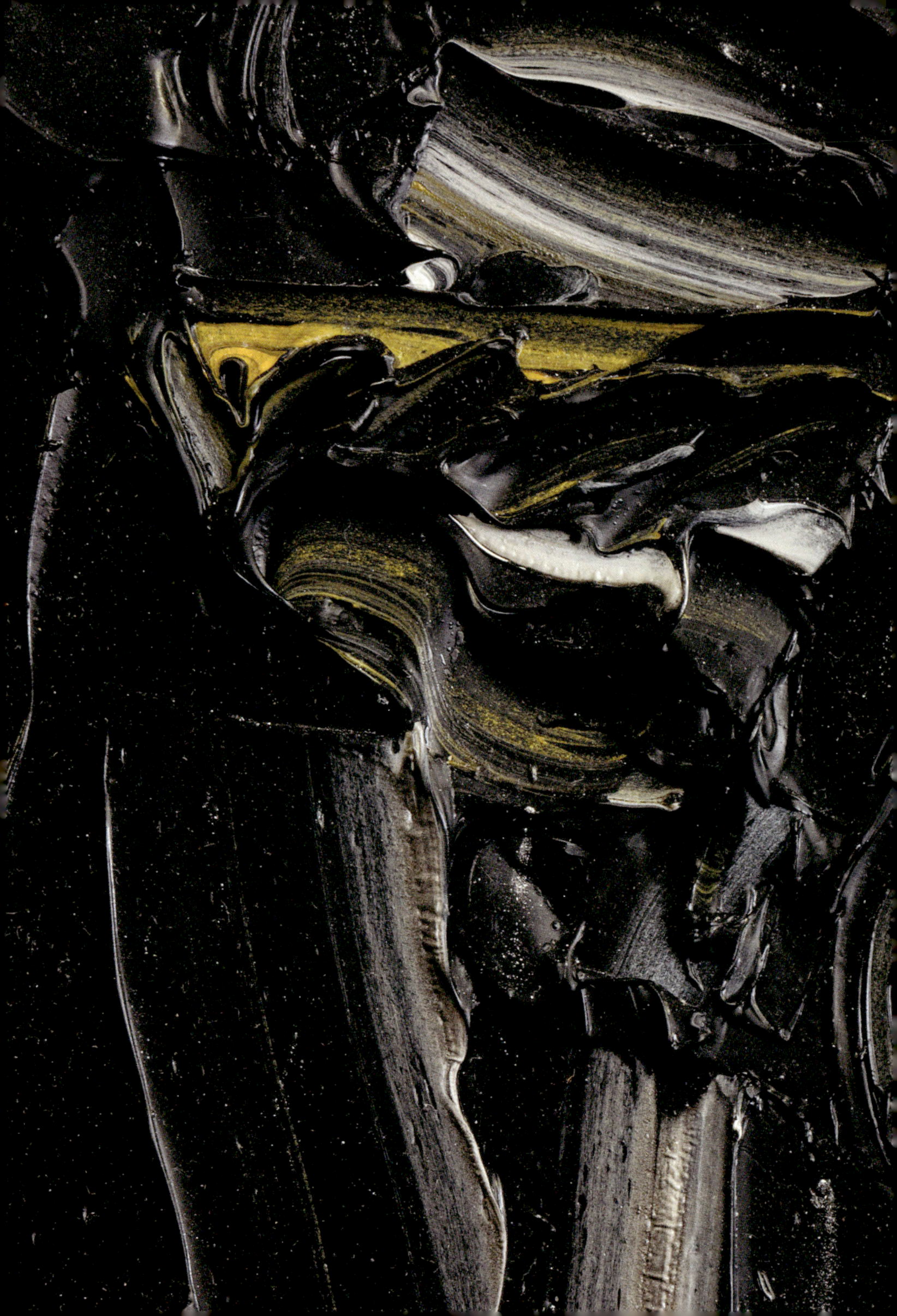

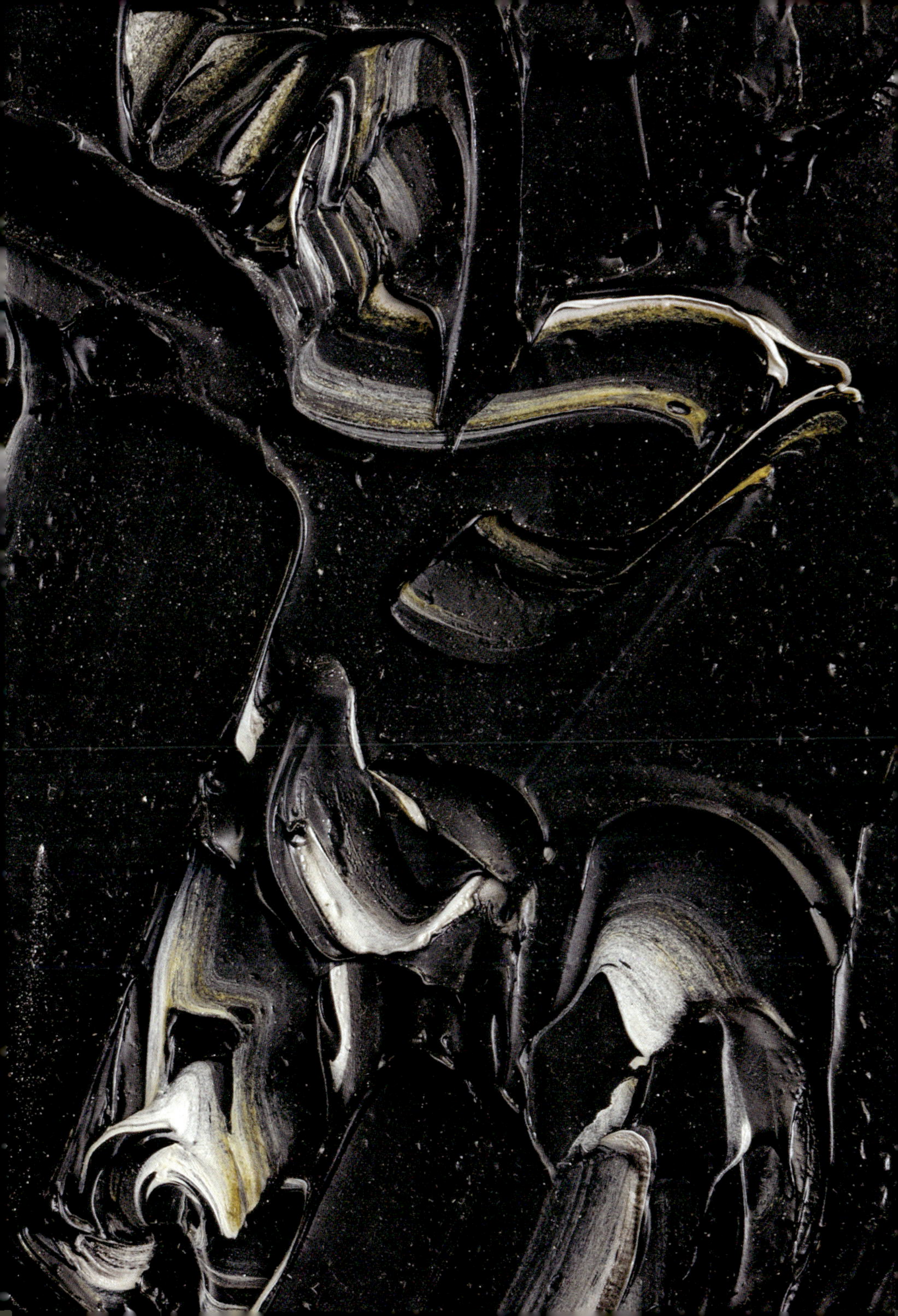

Hate must taste very good,
For its saccharine dust to linger
At twilight when darkness falls,
Or for its scree and vinegar bite
To tempt a father as a baby cries.
One would think a diet of rocks
Not enough to void other fruits,
But the glands still salivate,
And that iron acid twang of blood
Swells and feeds the appetite,
A talus of poison for lifted spoons,
Eager, yes, eager, to be drunk.

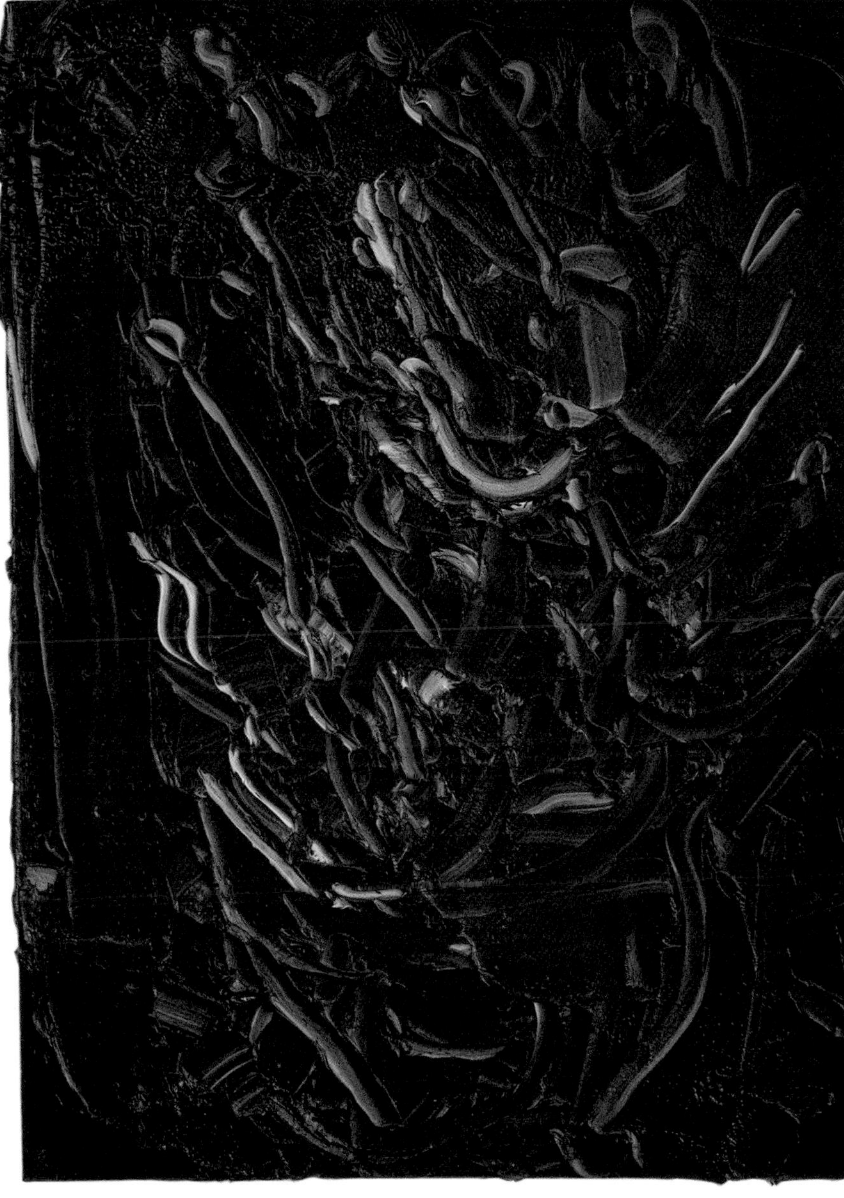

I find, when trapped, I can tell a coherent story of justice.
Meeting your red eyes, I counter with a tale, flowing
Smooth as thickening ice cream in a revolving churn.
Meeting your burnt hair, I tell you of my actions,
Of meetings in private, my wrapped heart of chocolate,
My earnestness and empathy for your exposed ribs.

I find, when trapped, I can dance a dance of gilded fear.
Meeting your strained neck, I can waltz through my books,
The poems I can recite for you, passages salted to my taste.
Meeting your broken knees, I can fold mine under me
To pray with you, shout to God as the tension slowly subsides,
And I continue my story, meeting your back, as it walks away.

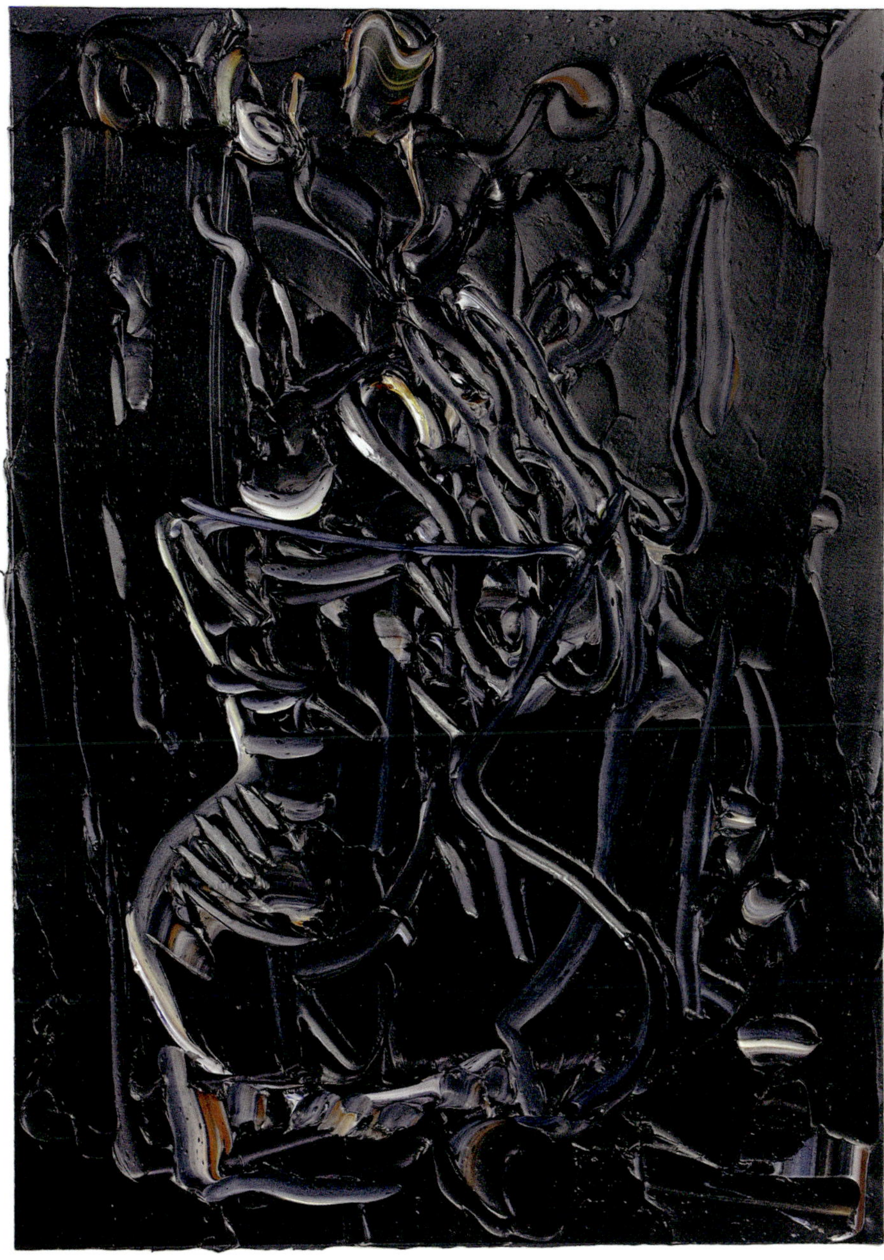

Those days, I'd pant as my air released,
Fled my mouth, shocked out by the heat
Glowing red on my skin, my finger pressed
On the surface showed a cooked steak.

Those days were hard, hard for anyone,
Harder for the old, bored and open for the young,
The heat was enough to drain your fight,
Cause the muscles to fail and the mind to clinch.

It went on for weeks, a humid malaise,
Dry mouths, empty hearts, step by aching step,
Highways and roads and rivers, live oaks full
Of crying cicadas and the dogs belly up.

And the norther would come, blue and black,
Running towards us, rising tall and scary,
Lightning heaven at the afternoon break,
Now cool enough, in the shade, to dance.

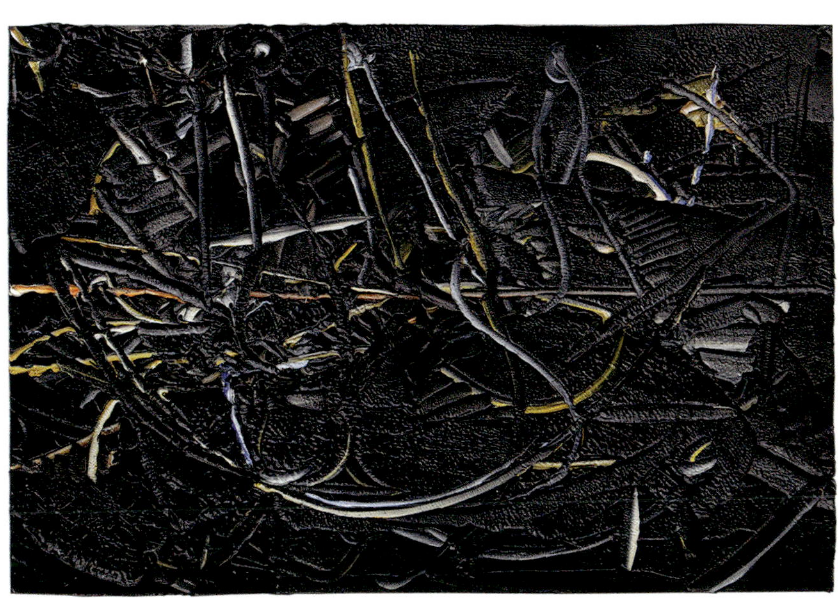

We breathe from underneath the mud,
Our hot dioxide bubbles gasp out upward
As our unseen signs to passersby,
Who walk upright and curse the soles
Of their shoes mucking the sludge of our home.
Insects intrude on us, small bugs dancing
On our faces, in and out of our nostrils,
Tickling their tents, our giving passages,
And causing us to shiver hard and tremble.
Ants wait for our mud to dry, just enough
To tunnel through the cracks for the same straw
We count as our dinner, supplemented
With protein when the same ants wander
Into the chasms of our digesting mouths.

They never teach their children how sharp
Our teeth can be, how our air can be poison,
How the mud can shake unexpectedly with our strain.
No, they cannot remember; they wander in,
Into the dark, one more, still one more,
Again, onto the welcoming plain of our tongues.

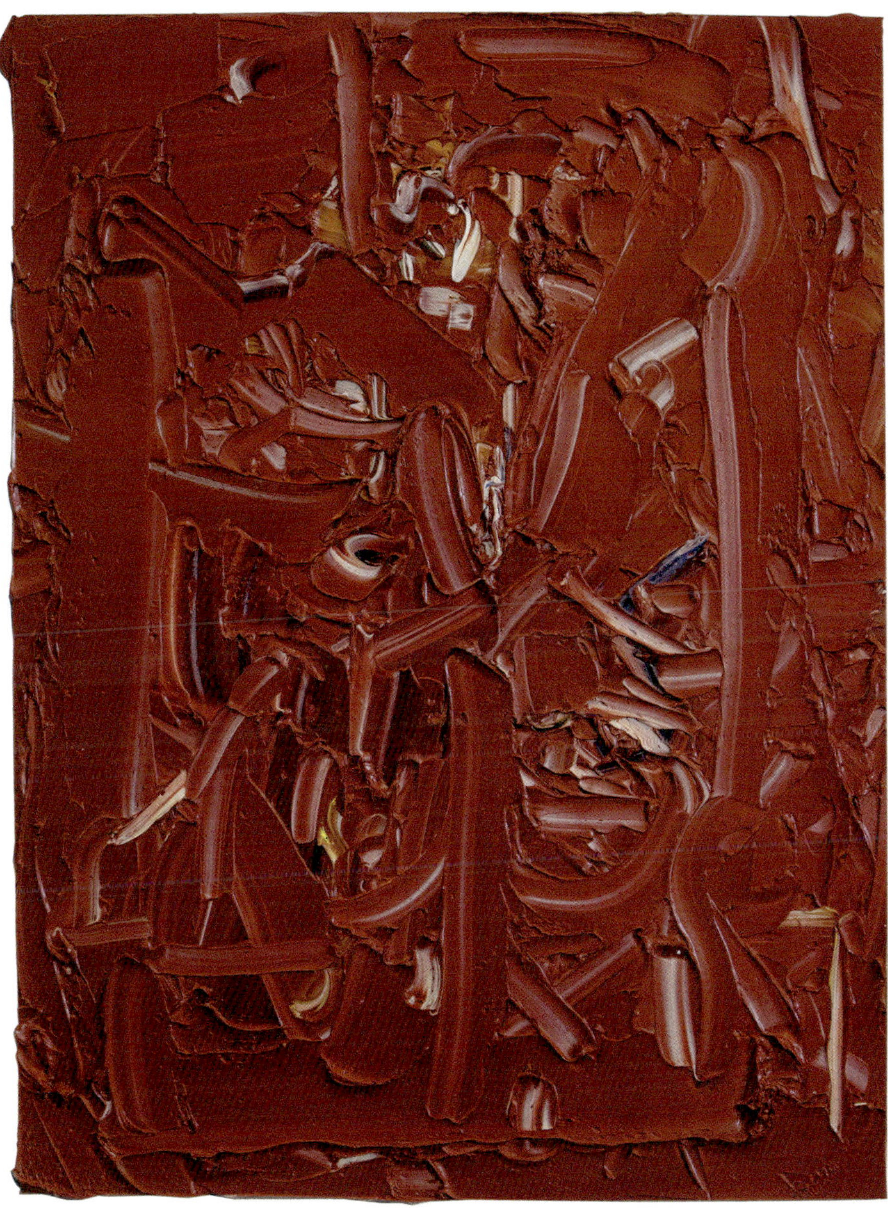

What we knew of her was two eyes, looking up from a burrow —
The details of the subterranean structure, the layered burdens torturously
Opening that secret tunnel and holding the walls, were invisible.
We simply saw her eyes vanish below when the rain came.

We stood over her, she would rarely surface, we called out,
Crying angry, only to hear the twisting below, her joints cracking loose,
Her fingers, her shoulders, her back, she always the one fleeing,
Us accusing, as though she recoiled by increments from our dark star.

None of us imagined how terrible that dirt could be,
We did not ask how each hot breath sunk her deeper
Into the habit of panic and fear, no light above to seek,
Only voices, no longer recognized, moaning out in her night,
Echoing other voices from her unspoken deep.

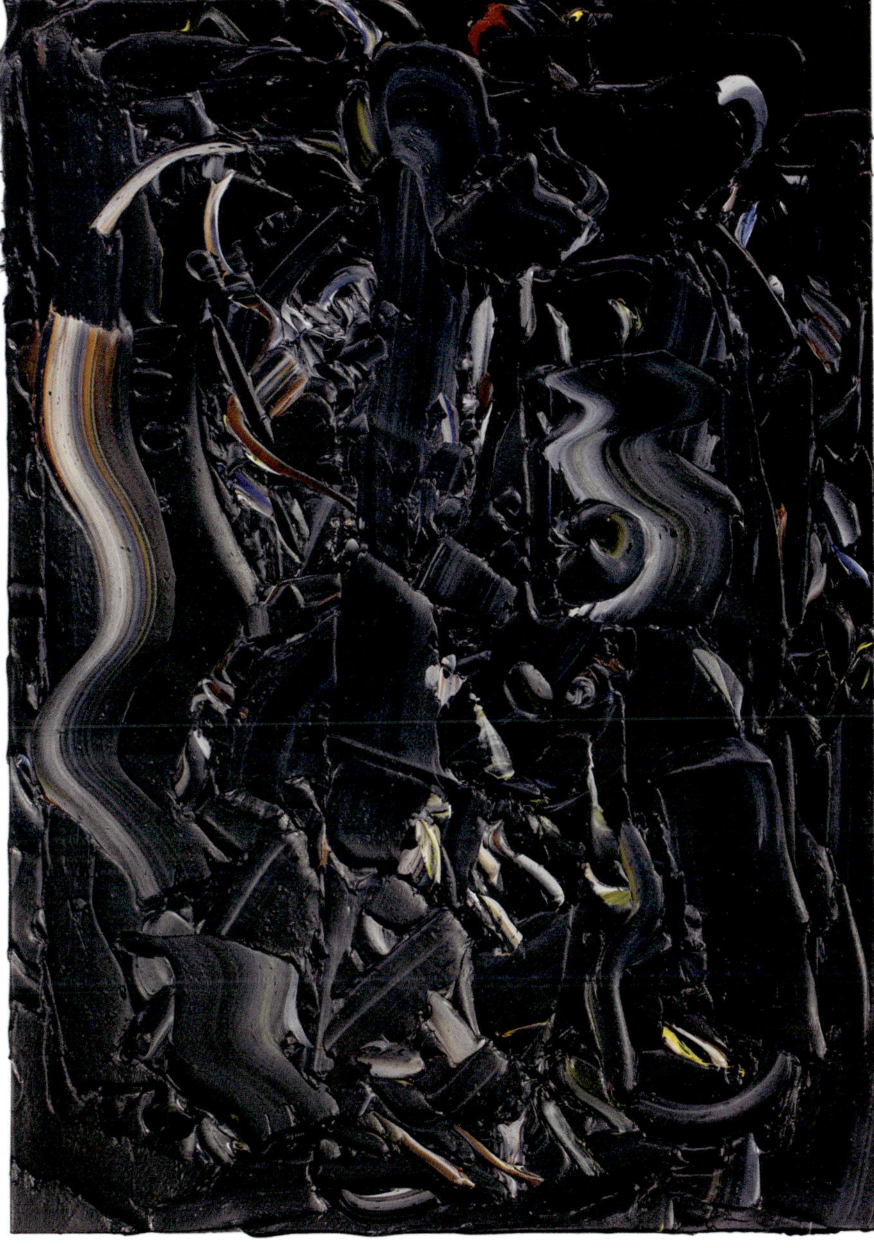

Under a refrigerator lamp, looming distant on the shelf,
A block of butter, the inscrutable heart of the kitchen.
I removed it from its keeper, onto veined Formica,
To sit like nothing else around, throbbing yellow in low light.
I thought of a dull knife, but the knife was wrong,
So I placed my hands around the mechanical curves,
Pressing gradually into the moisture, closing my fingers
To spurt the fat and oils graphically out into the air.
The glob turned into a slather with lumps to squeeze,
All turning warm and the warmth the warmth of me,
My substance, not of clay but of churned skim of milk,
A toss of salt and molecules, now energetically
On my face, onto my chest, down into my joints, over
My legs and knees and toes, everywhere, a joyful mess.

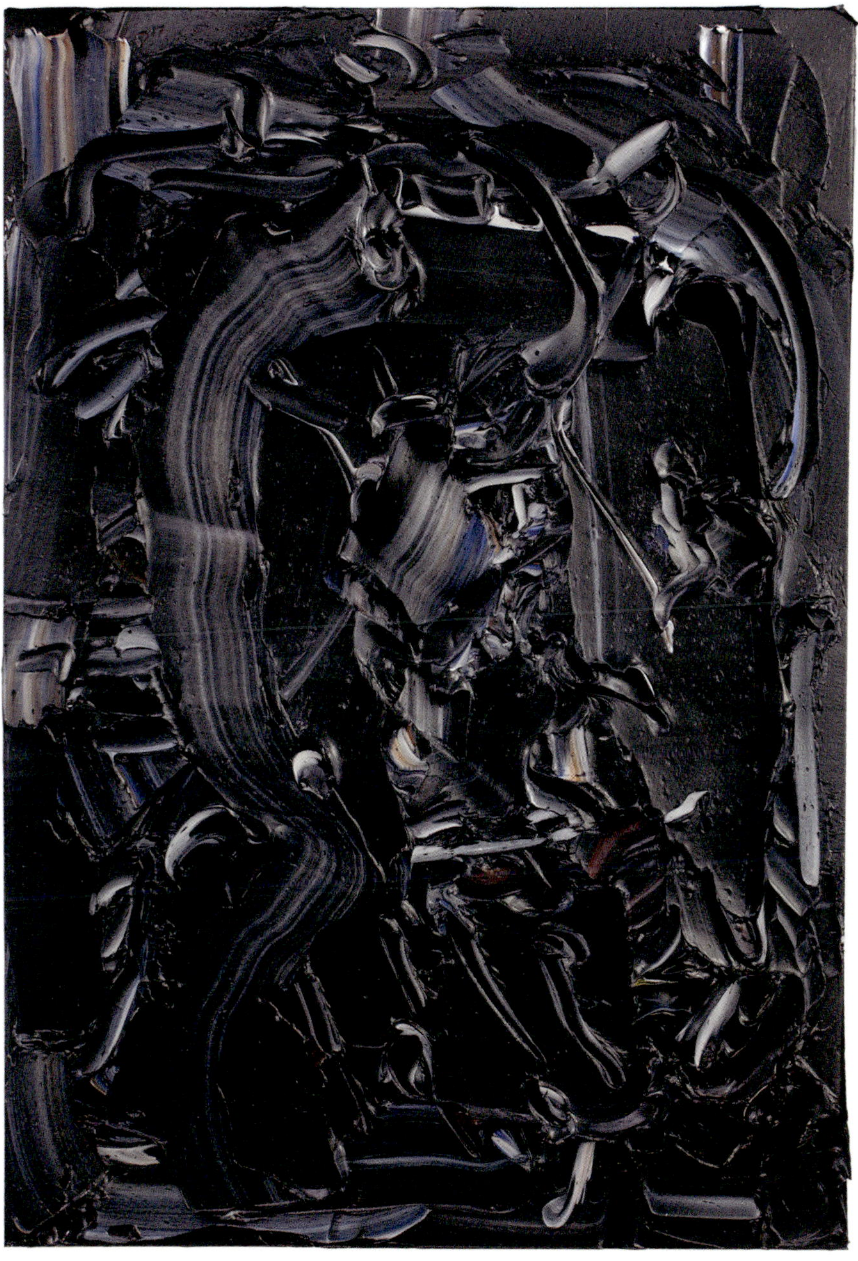

Blue pandemic, empty over Highway 40,
Navajo corn sky, drapes down, blue minds,
Bluish lips, Tangled Up in Blue, blue refrigerators
Behind hospitals, blue masks in the grass.
One morning in June, a navy Neil Diamond
T-shirt in the birthday mail, another shirt,
Ordered in mid-night at midnight, arrived in black.

Instant blue over the fields, riven and shattered
By gold electric strikes then pitter patter rain,
Marian blue monochrome, mom's favorite color,
Blue sharpie marks filling calendar days and months,
Blue Mesas on isolated desert pages, petrified trees,
A slice of blueberry pie on a blue plate,
Divers dead in a hundred caves at the Blue Hole,

One blue candy in the Blizzard, my Dad in a blue shirt
Under that blue sky, on the porch, stop the blue.

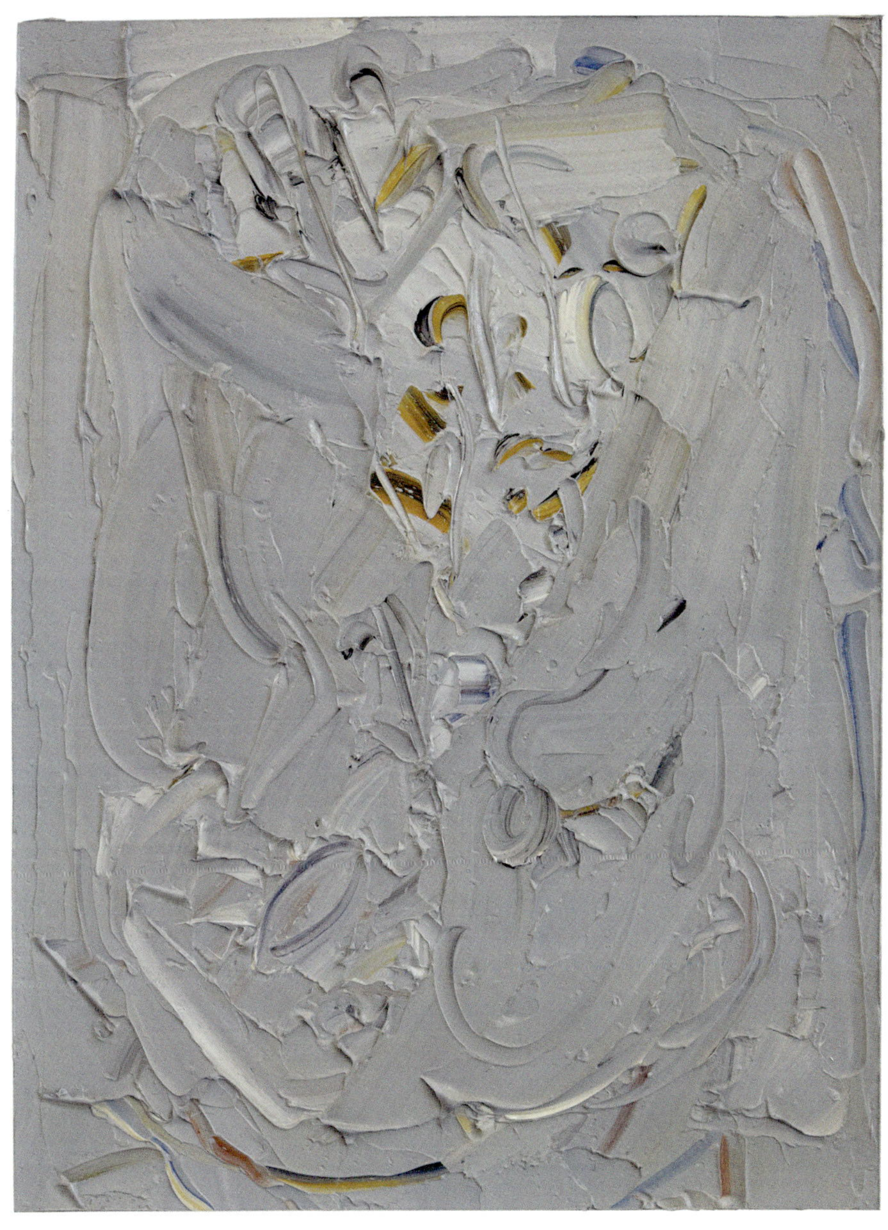

I sat upright, a statue
Straight-backed in the mirror,
Drawing myself over and over,
Able to be thickened or thinned,
Filled or erased, my contours
Capable of expansion or collapse.

I had been planning an altarpiece,
With myself as the central image.
In place of God, I offered my posture,
A magnanimous smile and visage,
And a niche held this familiar body,
Brazen on a heathen pedestal.

A divided word entered my mouth
And moved out of my mouth,
A radiant collage, a patchwork disc
Of woven wheat, wet with confusion,
A chameleon angel, a shapeshifting
Shadow staining my translated mass.

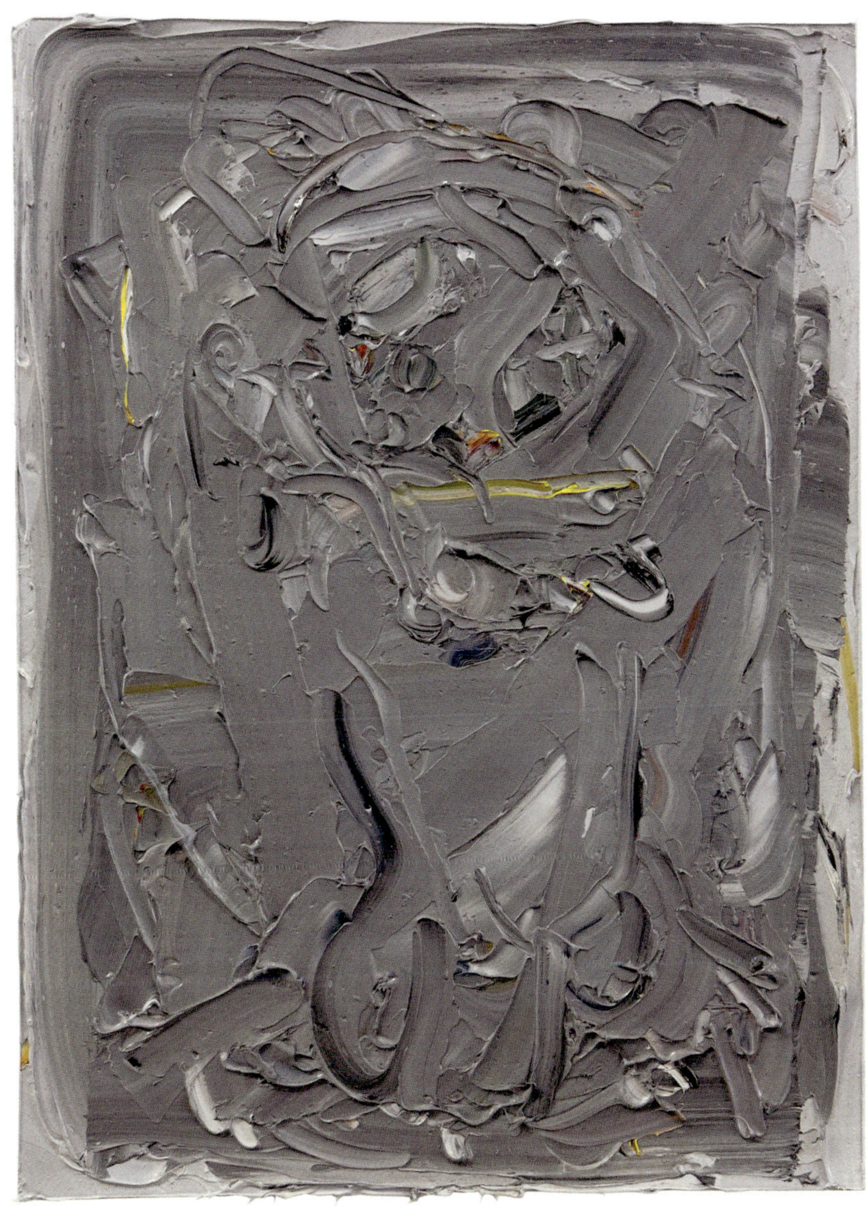

There's an orb of gauze and tape,
A beaten baseball of circling sutures,
With an ointment coat of pale green,
A layer of hopeful, spearmint balm,
Not yet able to dream its way to healing,
Expanding and contracting to the day's
Broken metronome of rhythmic pain.

There was a time this ball, tossed skyward,
Arched gently over in the air to speed
Down into a gymnast's hands, then up again
To float like an optimistic, nimble planet,
Above a series of elliptical flips, uniting in a receiving finish,
A practiced routine, an object working with flesh,
A concert of synchronicity set to folk music,
Two bodies meeting on an open, cushioned space,
Tied together in a ribbon of fragile grace.

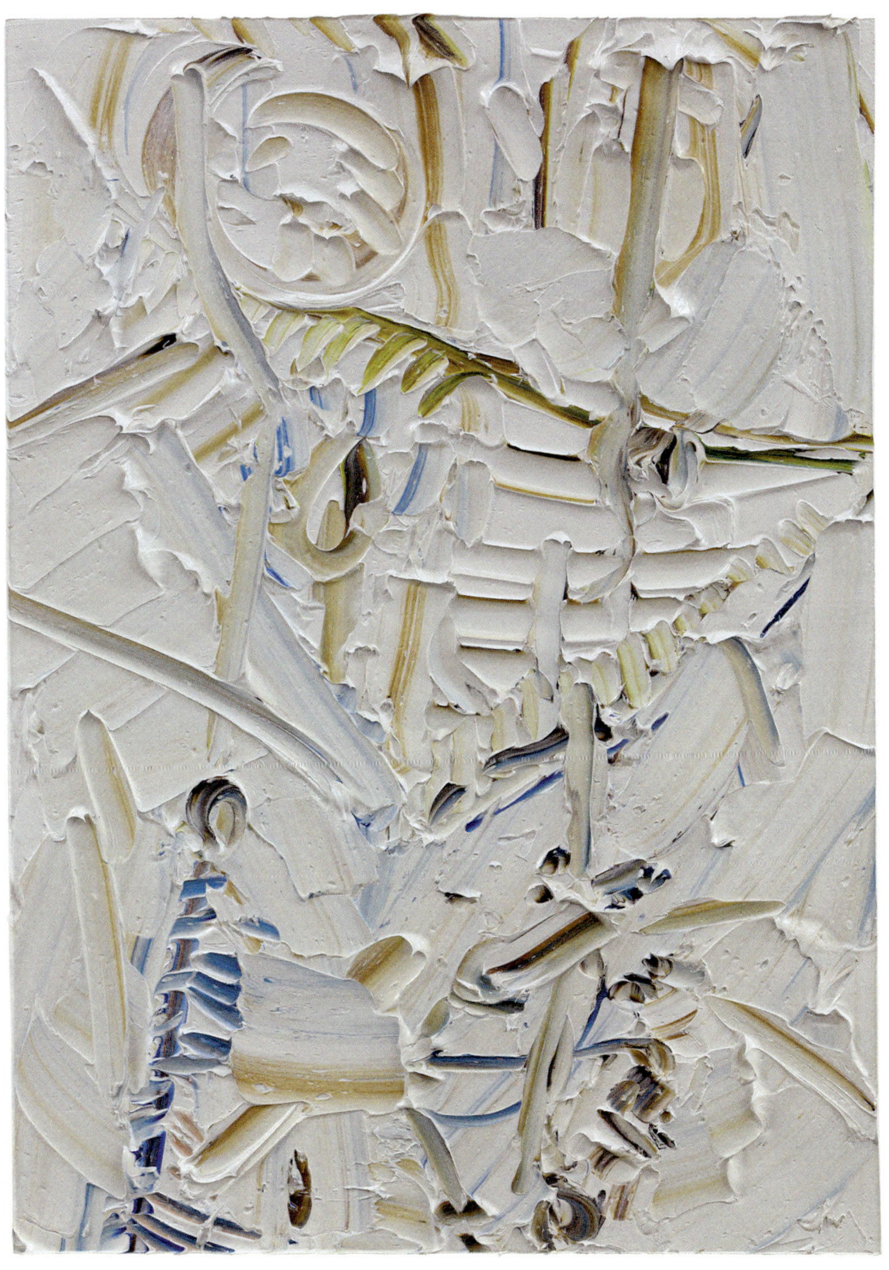

A canyon pulled apart by an etching river,
Boring and taking the rocks and rushing
Them away, mineral by mineral, to the sea.
One with the sky, a hawk soared through,
Of the same ancient entropic matter,
Eyes and hook, claw and feather down,
Red and sharp, carving an echo in the sky.

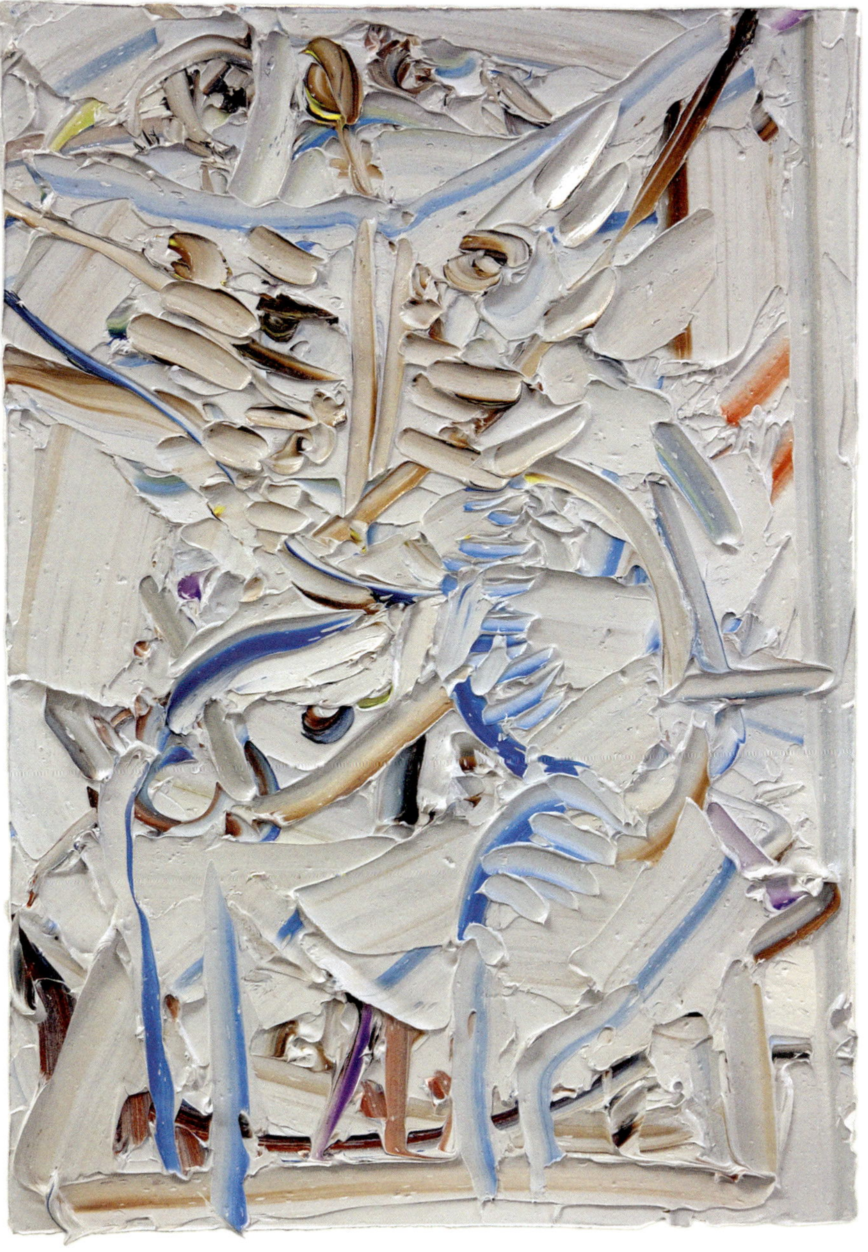

On an invaded bookshelf battlefield
With a Danish amputee legged table,
A couch with hand-picked upholstery
Formed an assaulted circle flanked by two upright chairs.
Across a parade ground of rugs, from wood floor hinterlands,
They marched out, visible gripping
Lidded cups and crackers, blocks and Legos,
A Kraken infantry of ruin with slim books and bears.
With flares of noise from blinking consoles,
Unrelenting and crazy, unformed and guerilla,
They volleyed victory at the towers of concern.

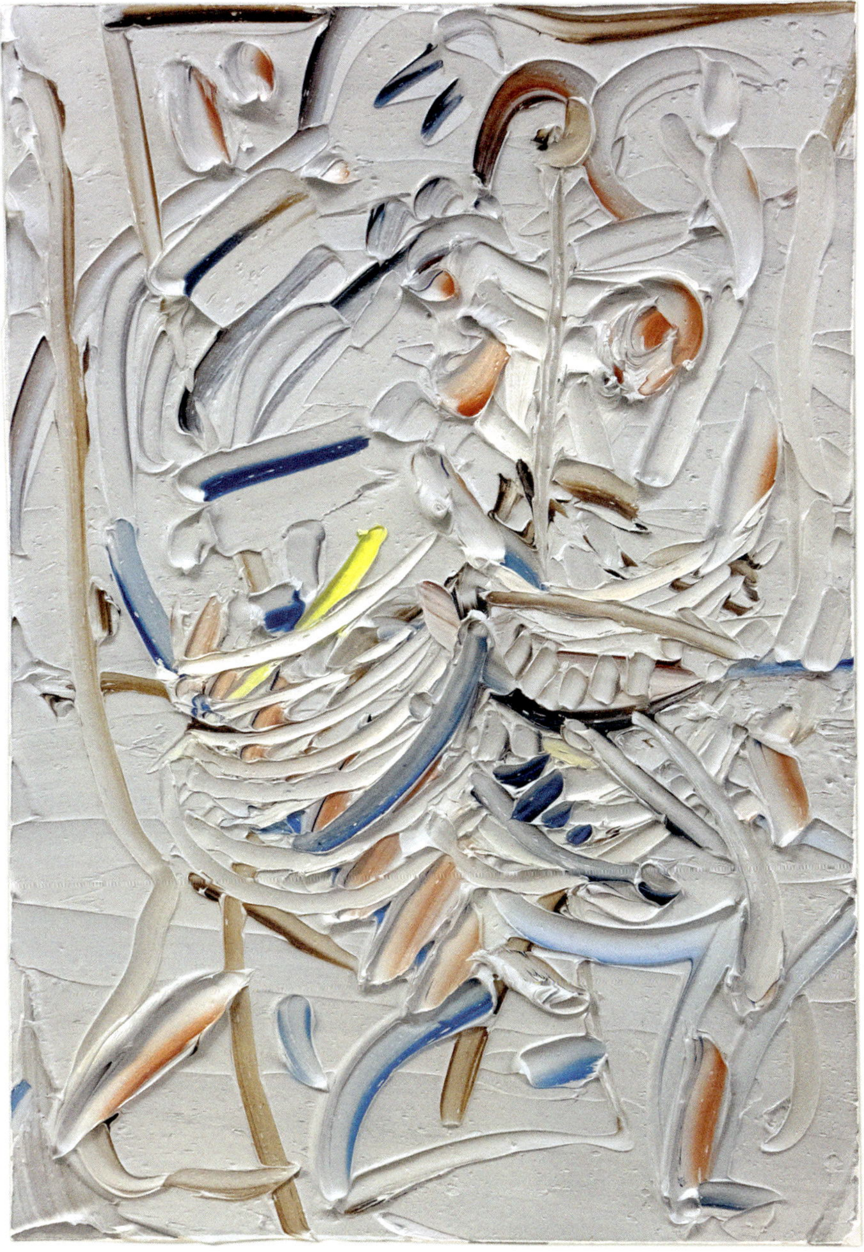

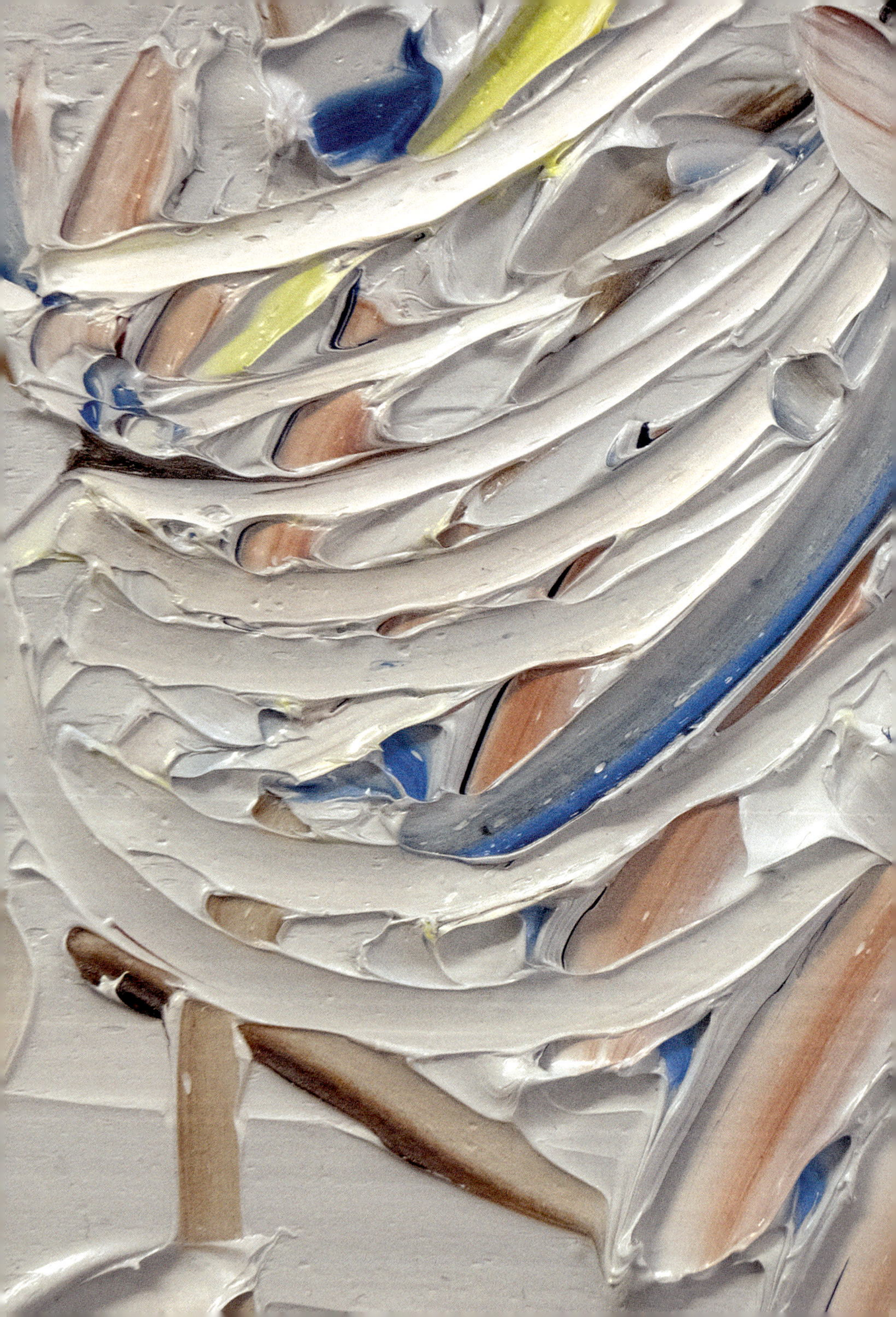

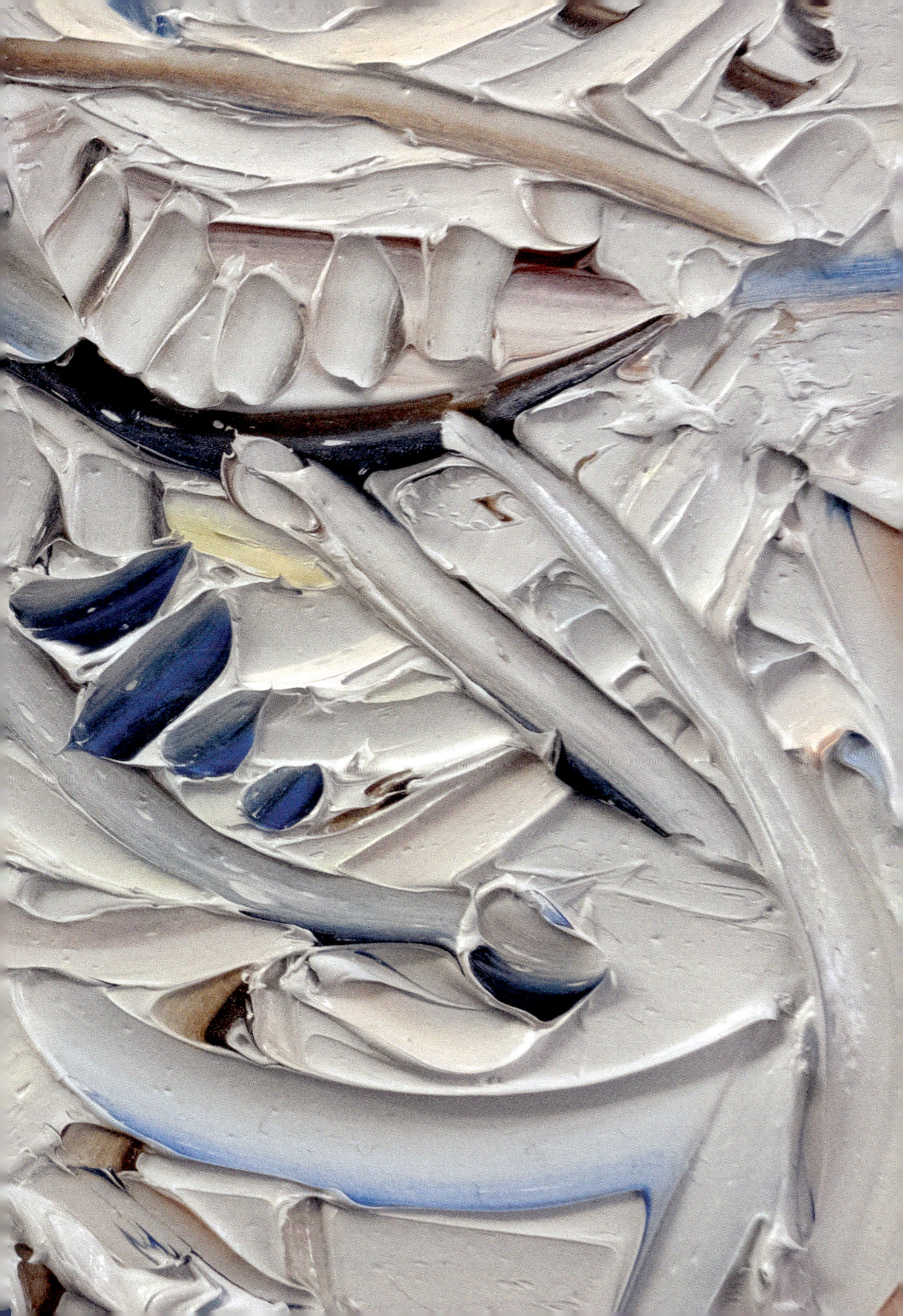

After betrayals, mistranslations, and plenty
Of stuttering aftermaths, I dissected the word
And laid its organs and bones on the table:

I + pif + ə + ni

The "I" who was, who walked upright
On a stacked spine, with young breath
Moving out and through like honeyed smoke.

"Pif," the heart in love and the mind curious,
And the "ə," the skid, onto muddy concrete,
Bloody knees sliding forward from the fall.

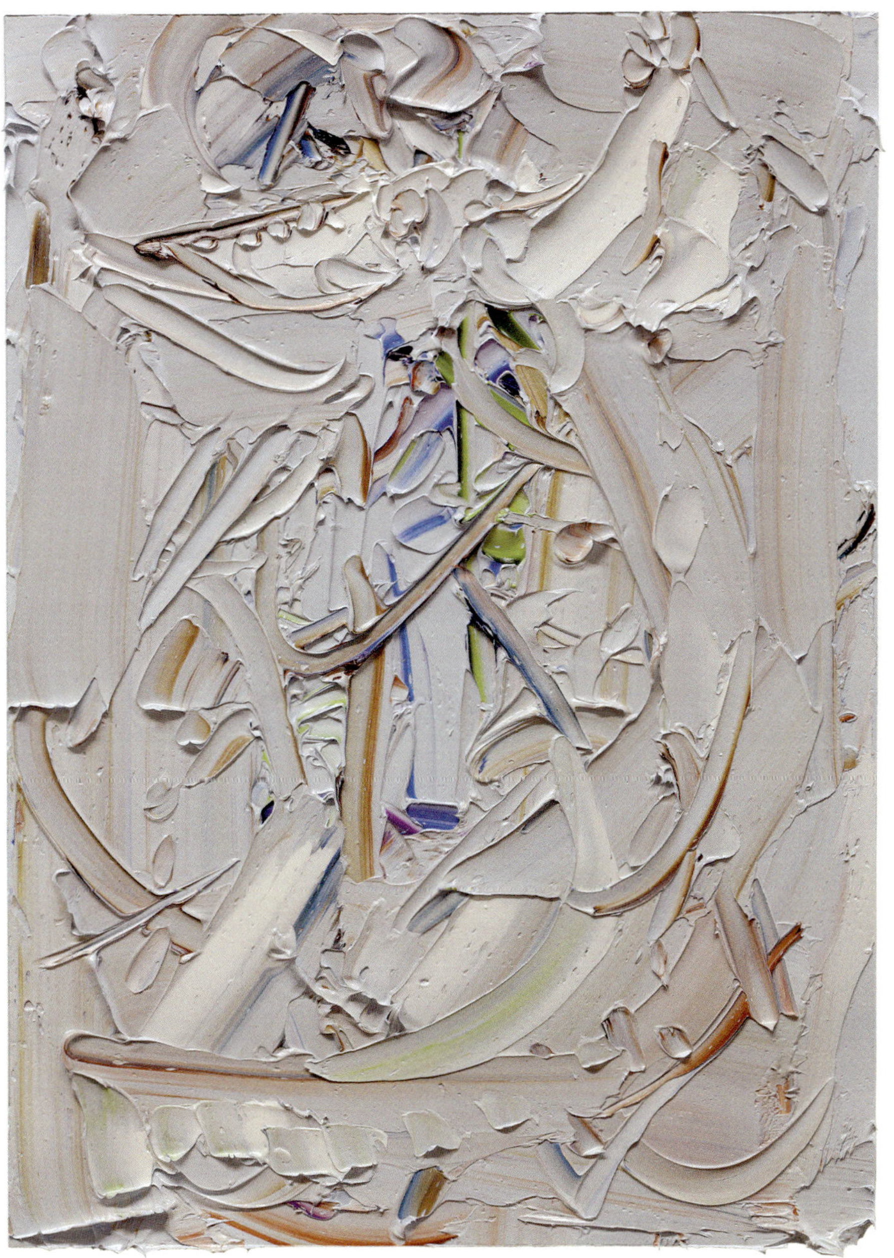

Durer at 32

Ahead was the death of his mother,
When winged creatures would flutter off
Of etched plates, to sit forever, head in hand,
Symbols dark and unable to use their tools.

But those prints were years away from this,
When watercolor dispersed a Virgin's treasure,
To every blade of grass, every numbered sparrow,
And every bud in a wide cathedral of turf.

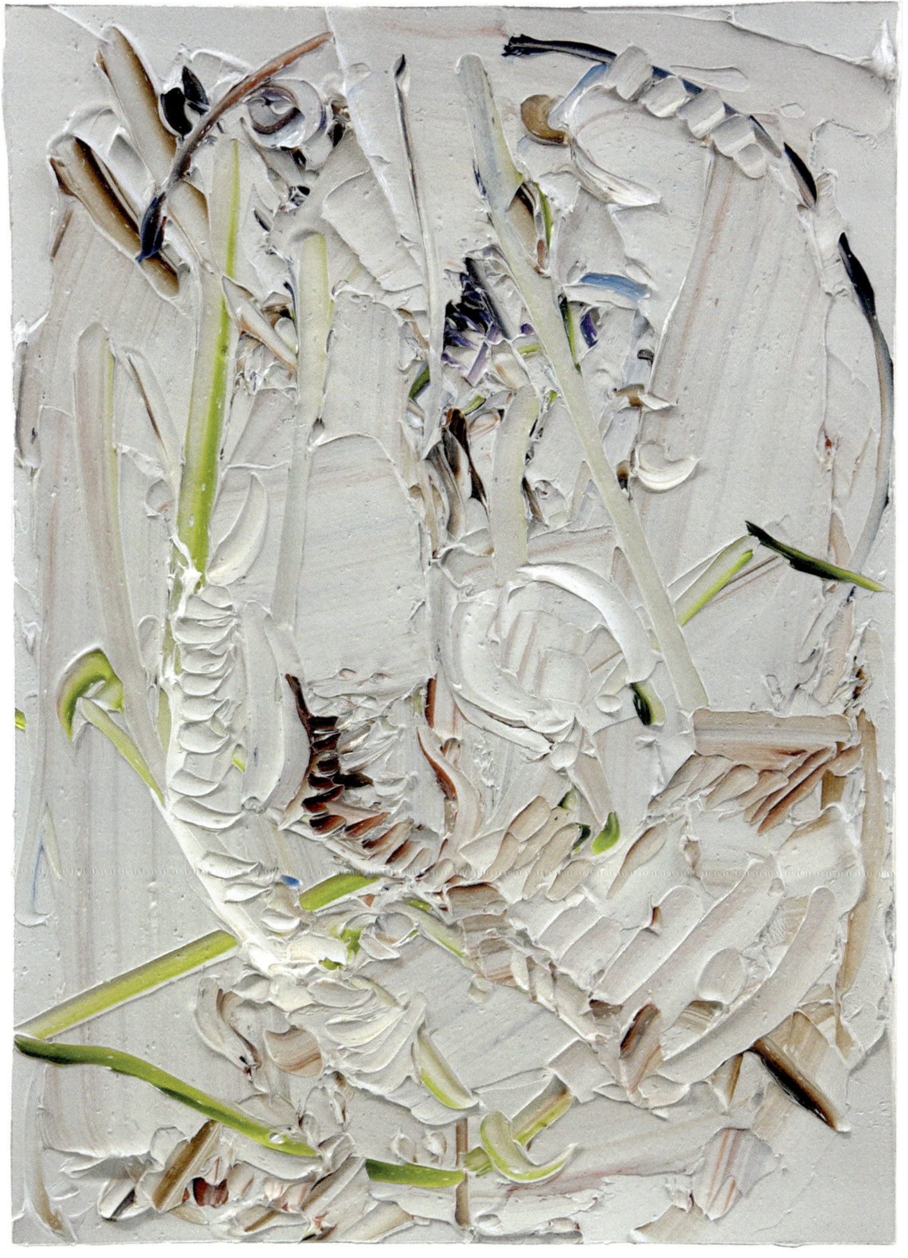

Where roofs were punctured
And marble burned, jewels
Were torn from the necks of corpses.

Violence had fought its way in, sacking
Sanctuaries and tossing lapidary
Fragments down to violate the crypts.

Only door lintels and posts remain,
To be believed again, trusted again,
Entered again from terrible fields.

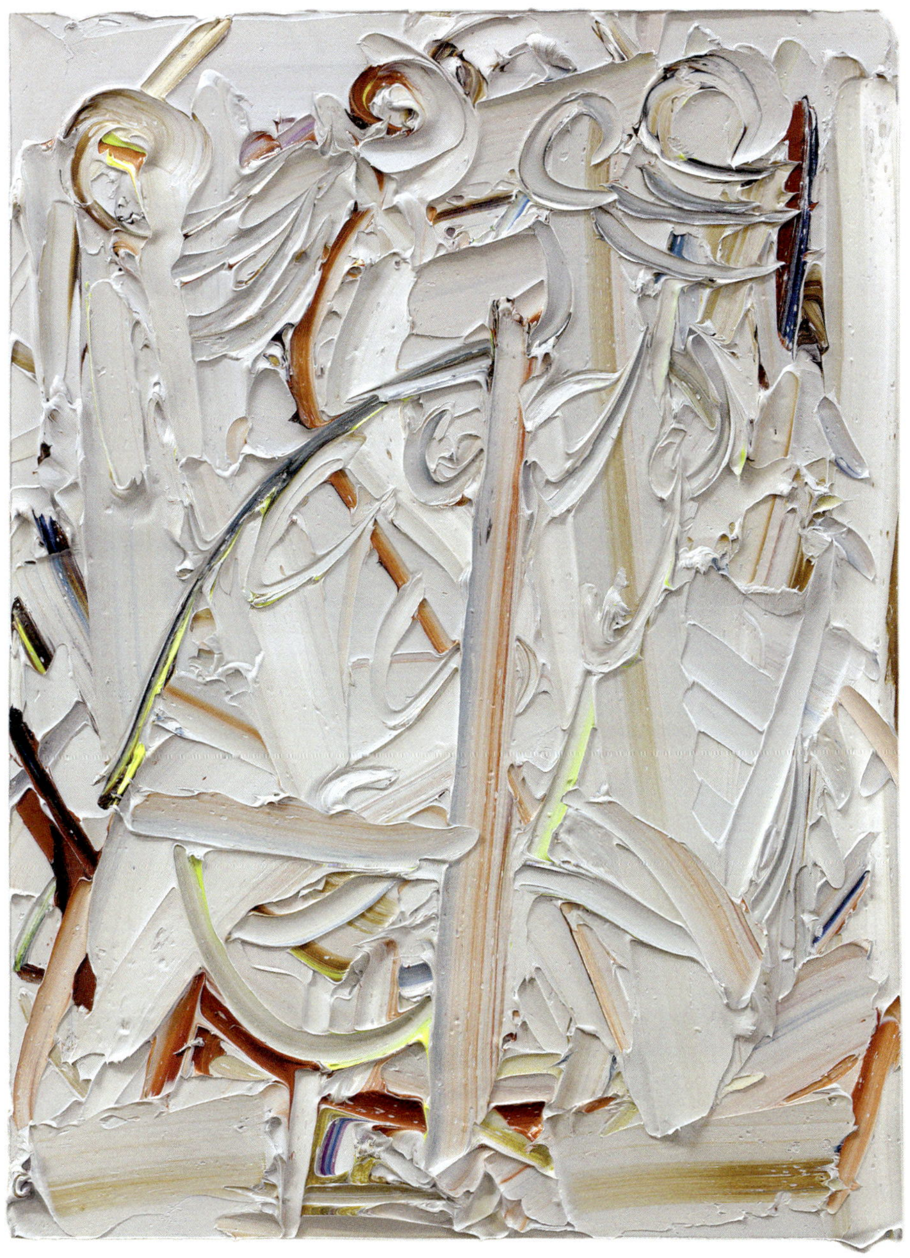

Up with confidence, the elders
Cast their names through the valley
Like lots against shards of stone.
See here, Patriarchs on thrones,
The temples, the pulpits of Zion.

Angels landing, thunder headed
Hives for God to rest his gold
And take his virgins through the gate.
A red streak on a rock face,
The altar, the sacrifice, substance
Of the certifying sword, now Utah.

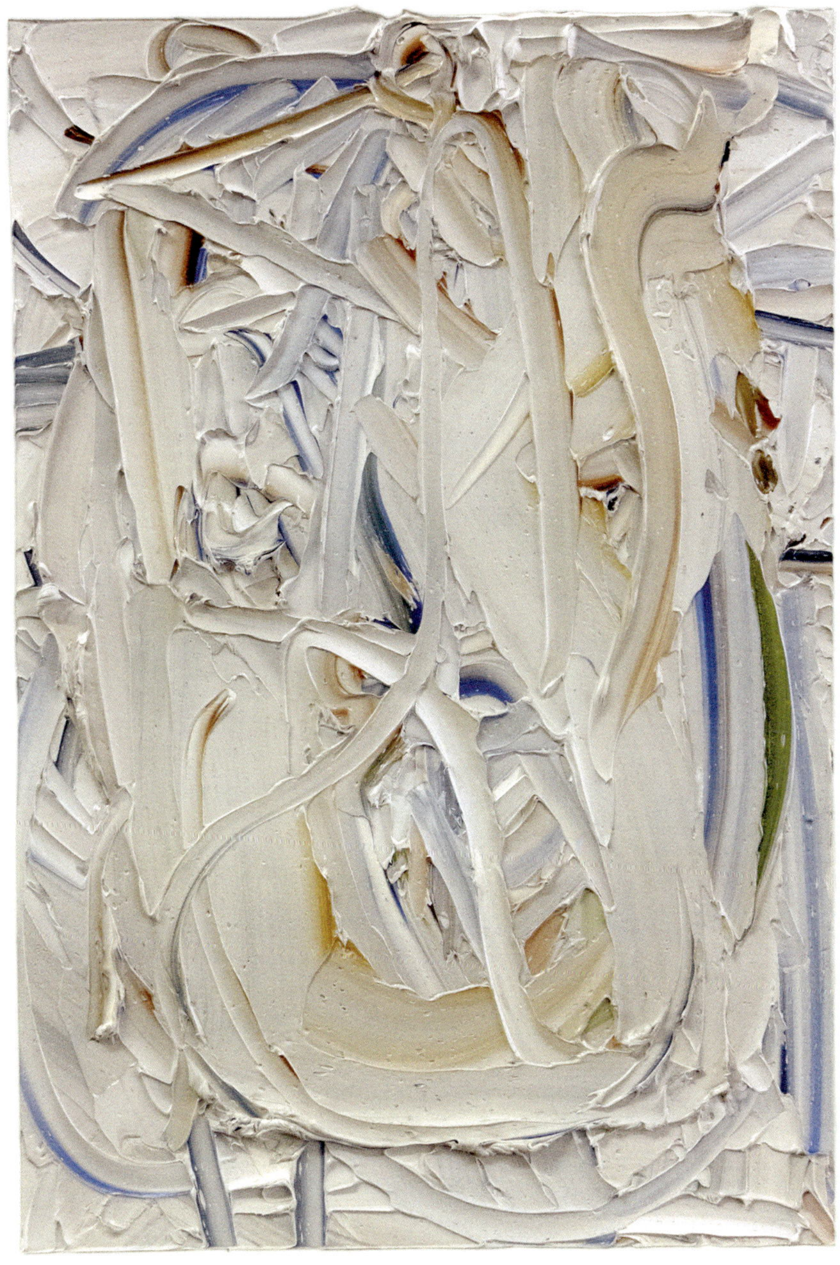

So swings the clarinet, thumps the bass drum,
The tuba farts to the dance of a ramshackle man,
Who extends his chest and puffs his person
Out from the soft foam jaws of a shark mask.
A bee in his brain, the bullet, his angry salsa
And contorting rumba, macarena twerking
Lunatic undulations of crotch, thrusting ellipses
And twirling swerves through a Parkay reef.
Up from his bubble, breathing comb-over oxygen,
He looks up and out, burning gold and emerald eyes,
Towards the inevitable sunstroked waves above.

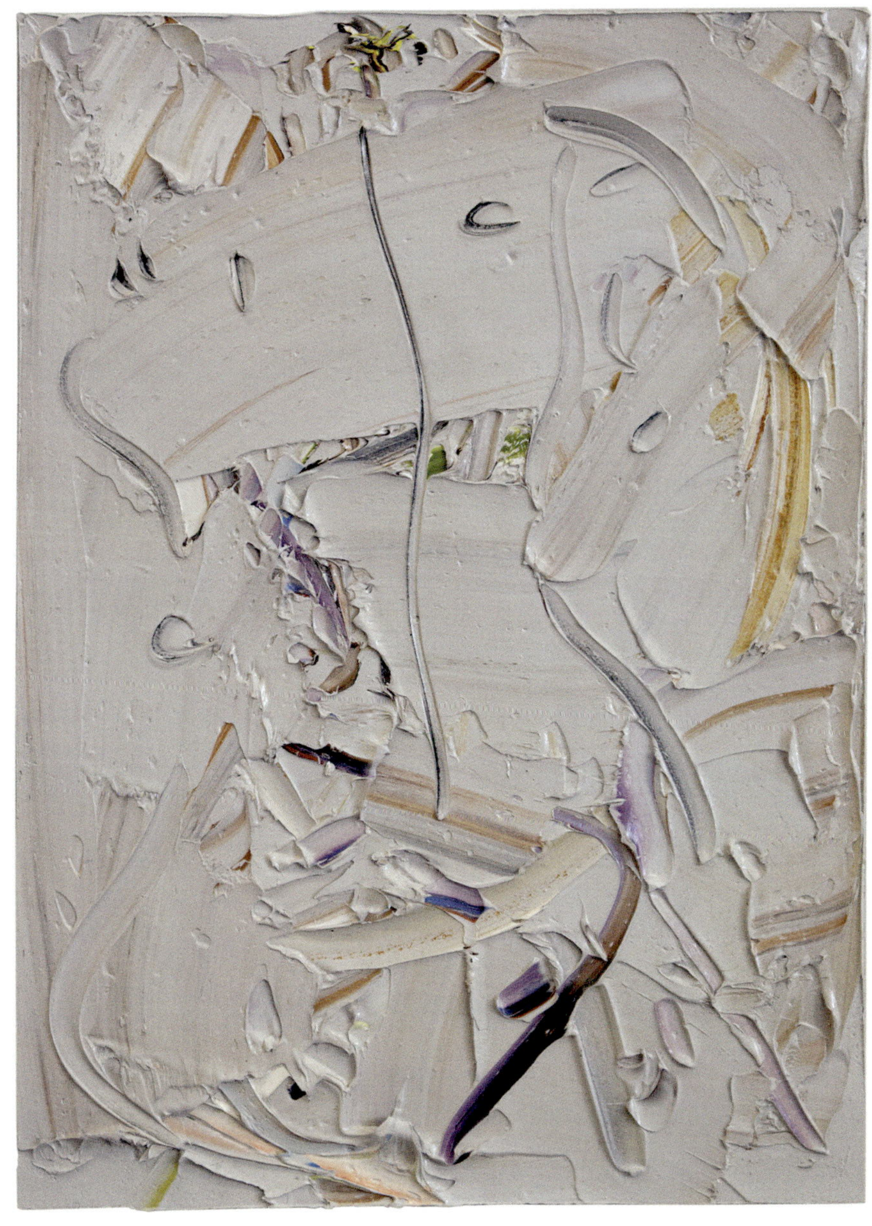

A boy, with a wet copy of Keats in his pocket, walks the city line,
From a provisional tarmac fringe of bubble wrap and cardboard,
Into stacked concrete towers, draped with laundry lines and plants,
Window unit walls and cell-like shrines of pop star posters.
He continues, from malted smells and emulsified tastes, across
Plains of touch, forests of sounds, then out to the eye's tomb:
Phantom images, phantom pains, thicker and heavier, in the city center,
Beaux-art, Deco into firm lines of glass, brutal, presumably beautiful.

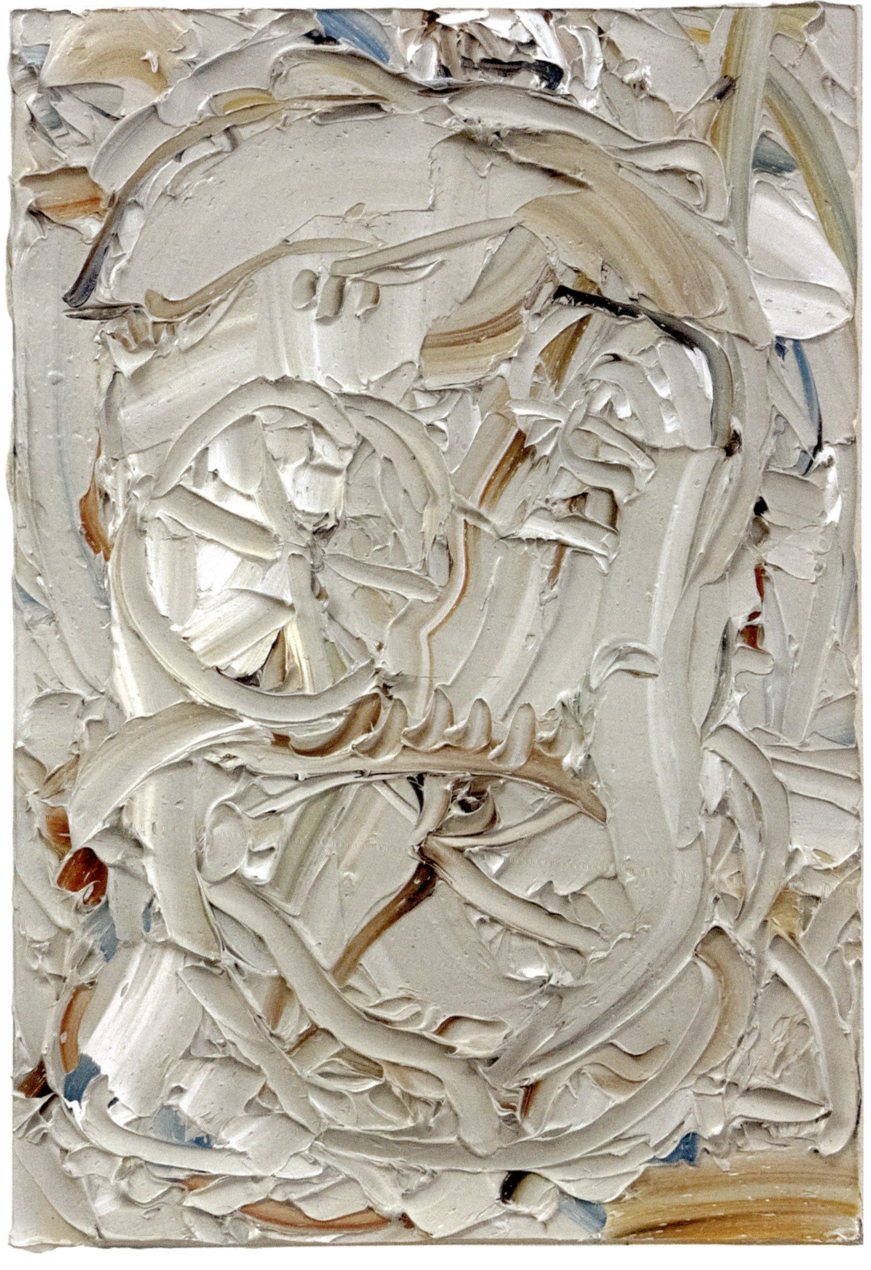

White gravel crunch
Sun struck metal
Sheeting radiating hot
Empty dry lipped
Silent scream locked
Waiting room agony
Powdered creamer
Eyes untethered
Flinging flying no
Runway, no landing
Lily fish flesh on fire
Eyes untethered
Dad is late, Mom is late,
All too languorously late,
That day a memory
In amber forever.

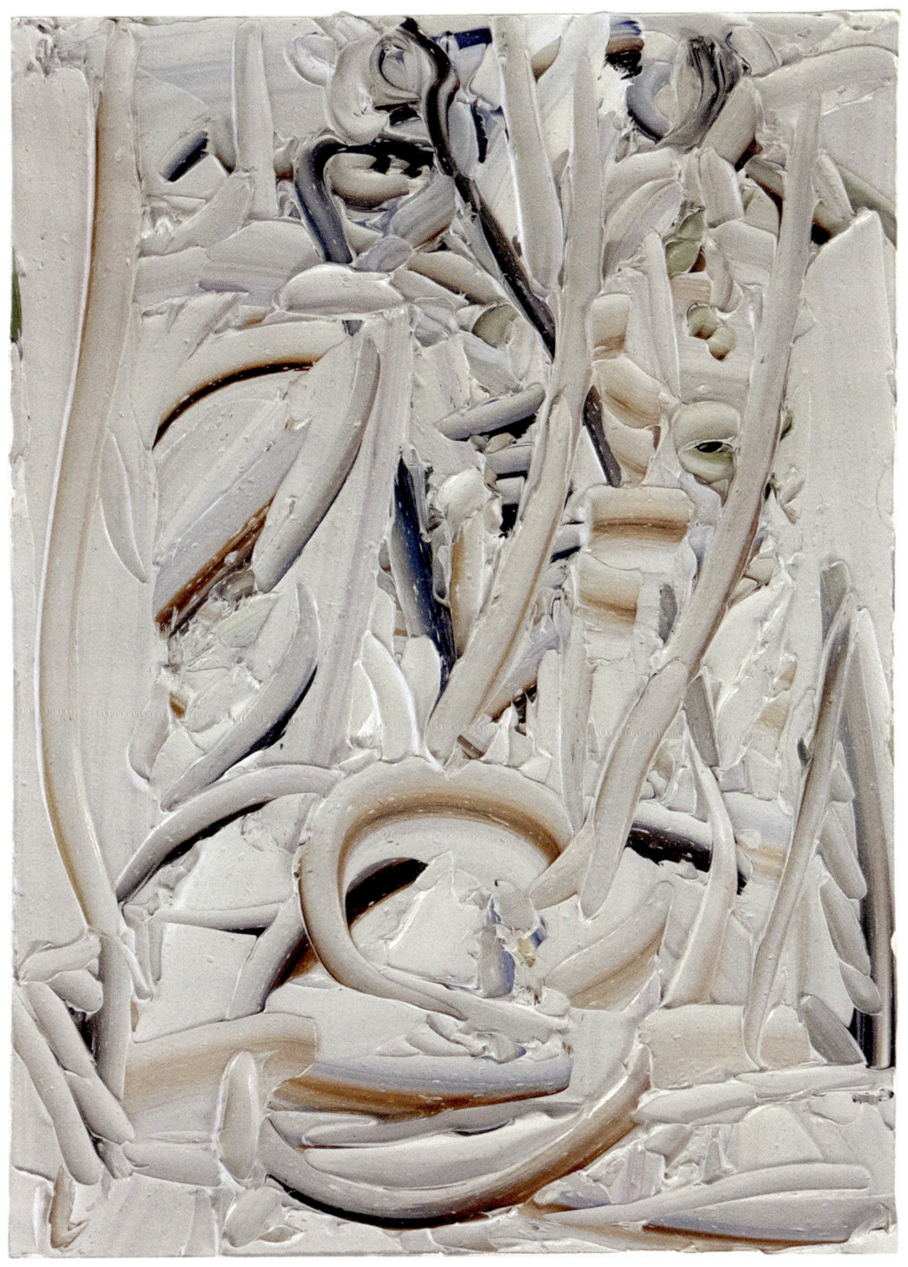

After the names were released,
Here's what we currently know:
Dahlia was a sleepy debutante,
Who loved large, ruffled skirts,
And Zinnia was out of time,
With her old-fashioned felt hats.

Iris had a sharp purple tongue,
Lily finished school projects,
With white glue and silk.
Hibiscus with her trumpet,
Hydrangea with her solarium of light,
Were all in Jasmine's soft circle.

It is hateful to know what we know,
That Amaryllis no longer puckers her lips,
That Violet mourns each of these cut stalks.

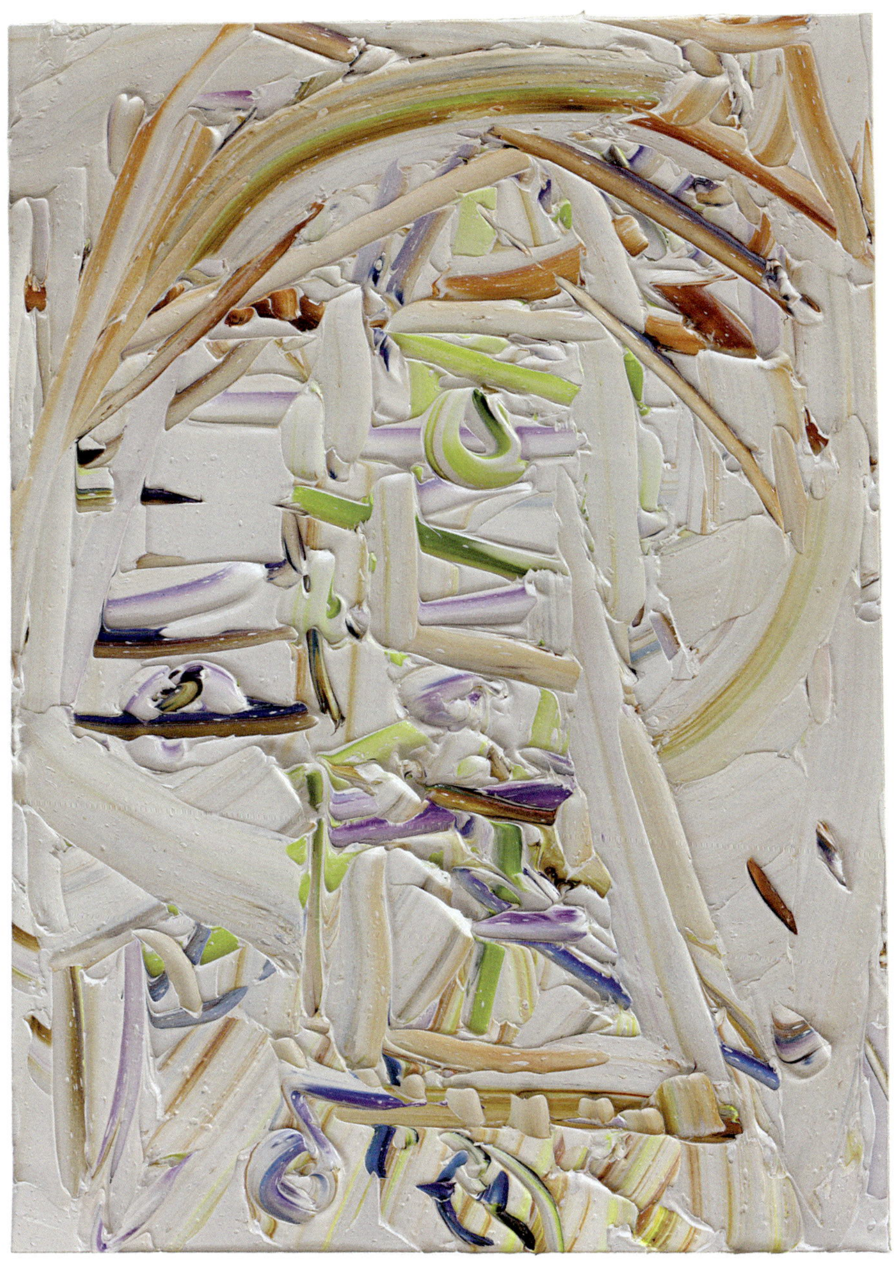

At the fenced edge of our farm,
A tilled field took the blended glow
Of our house lights into the night.
Plowed rows echoed into more rows,
Rippling far, harrowed flat, worked
Right after the bite of the first frost.
Out there, united with that dark,
A twist of red and yellow leaves,
Whirled with the winter wind,
Unable to rest on unplanted ground.

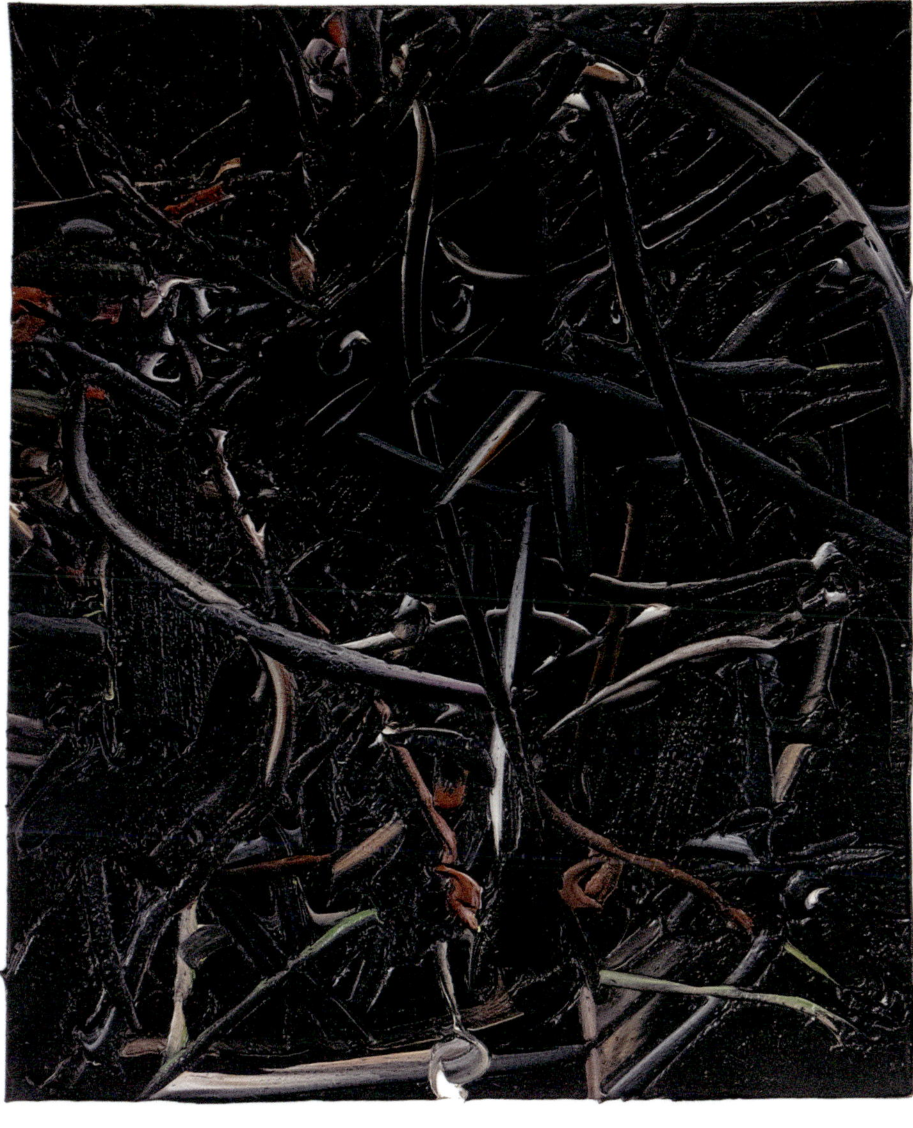

The shed had stored the season's grain.
Gradually empty sacks piled its floor
With fermenting leftovers from his last days,
His last feedings, the last bags of seed
He stacked then tossed to tight teeth.

Now the aftermath, the snakes,
Multiplying over the course of years,
Moving in the trash, their silver ropes
Twisting and terrible, their gunmetal tubes
Sliding and devouring in corn flour panic.

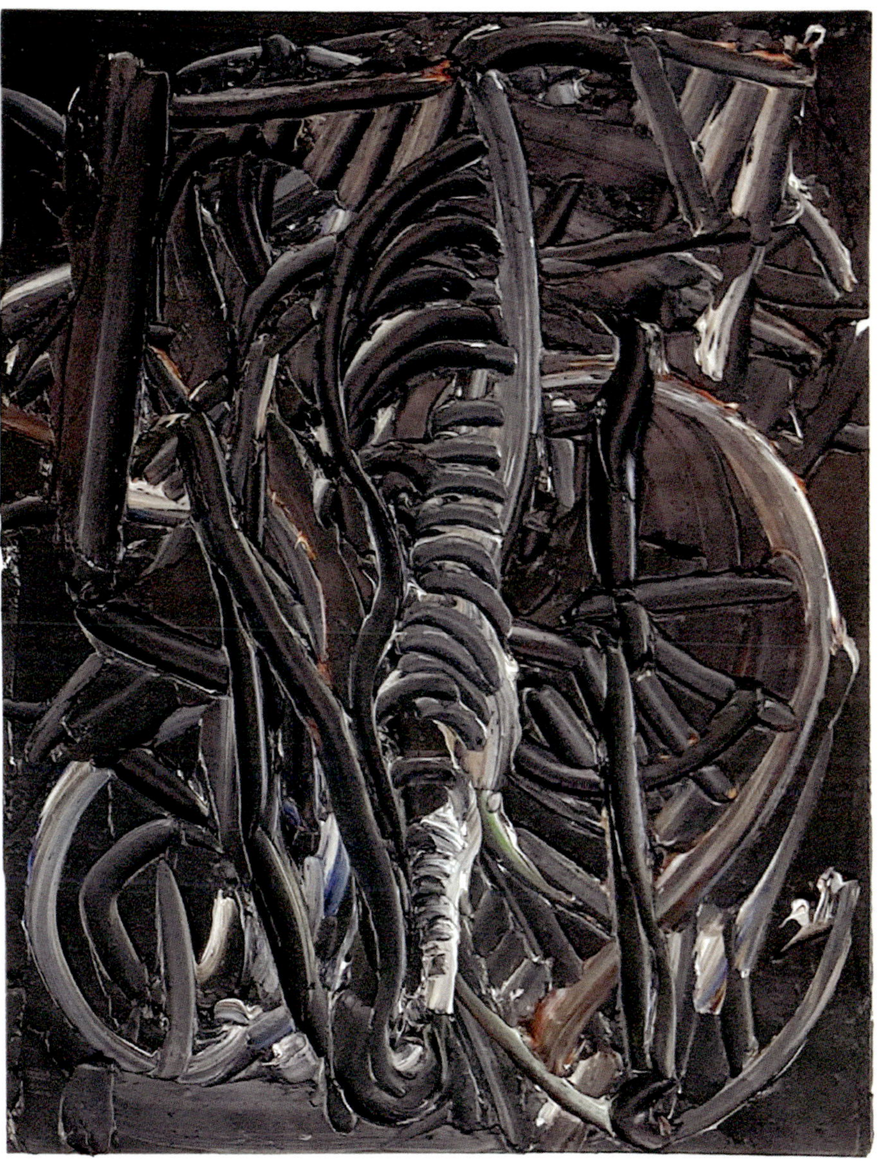

The house was too lonely, too abandoned to resist,
And there were no fences or dogs or memories
To impede my intrusion, though the reaching grass
And broken roof, loose floorboards and fetid holes
For snakes and rats, all made convincing guards.
Silence barred the door, reclaimed the field,
But voices were still there, somehow, in the ruins,
Of what they had wanted, of what they believed they owned —
A broad pasture, a shifting sky, a God who guided them.
I could join them, for now, in the rooms they built,
Off a road now paved, beyond the last school bus stop,
Where one had kept a box now covered in dust,
Full of blue imitation pearls, full of a cloud of white feathers.

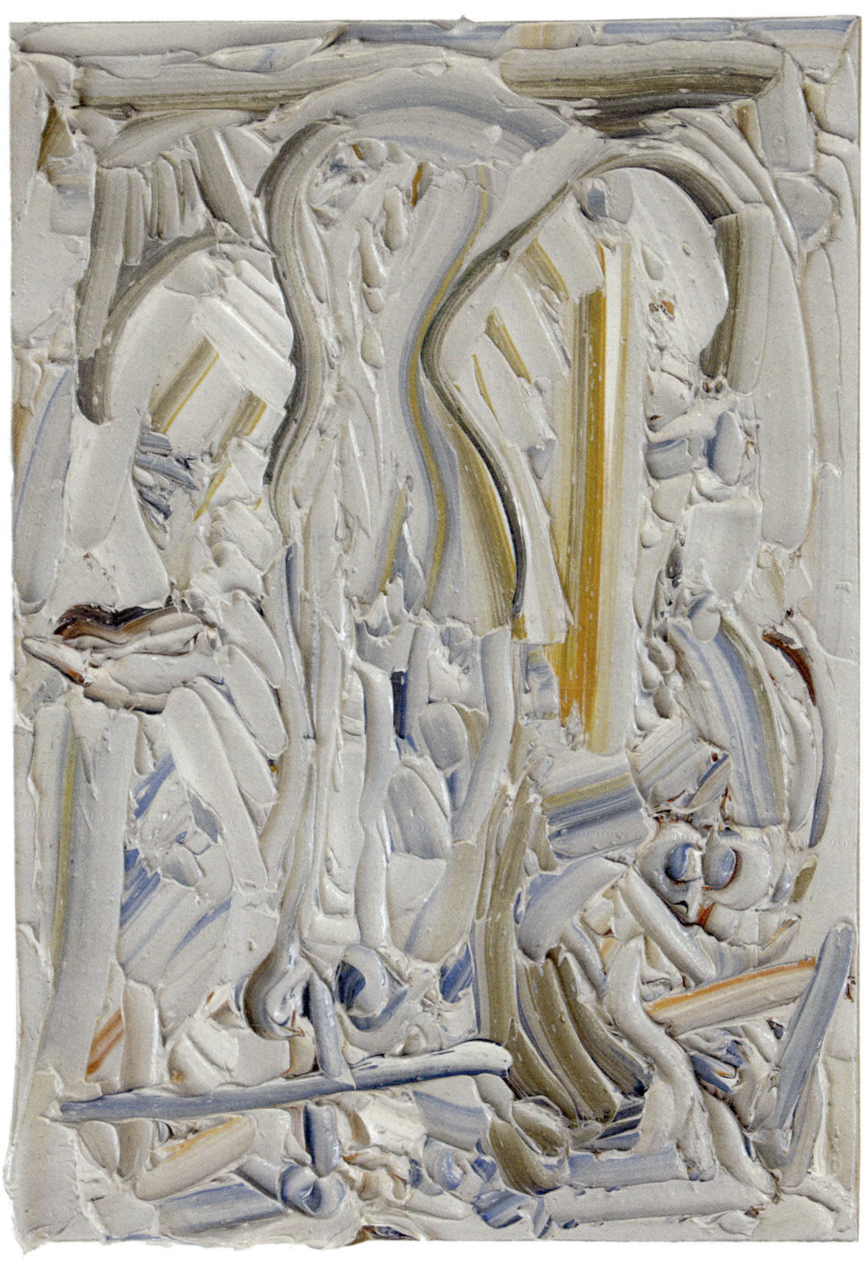

Our town had names for everything and everyone,
And the names were kept and looped in circles
Inside an established border, one to one, one to five,
Five out to a corroded and rusted edge of wire.
Ours was a world of accumulated tin and holes in tin,
And those without names would come with carts,
Raucous with tools swinging, with rows of massed jars
Full of viscera and cooked liquids, mushrooms and yeast.
They carried charcoal fires and grey water, used together
To build and dry clay dams around all the open wounds
On our plates and on our mugs, on our hammered out
Sheeted roofs and on our proclaiming shingle signs.
The strangers would pour molten metal into those molds,
And spitting air, they would blow and strike
And seal the tortured leaks in our shallow cups.

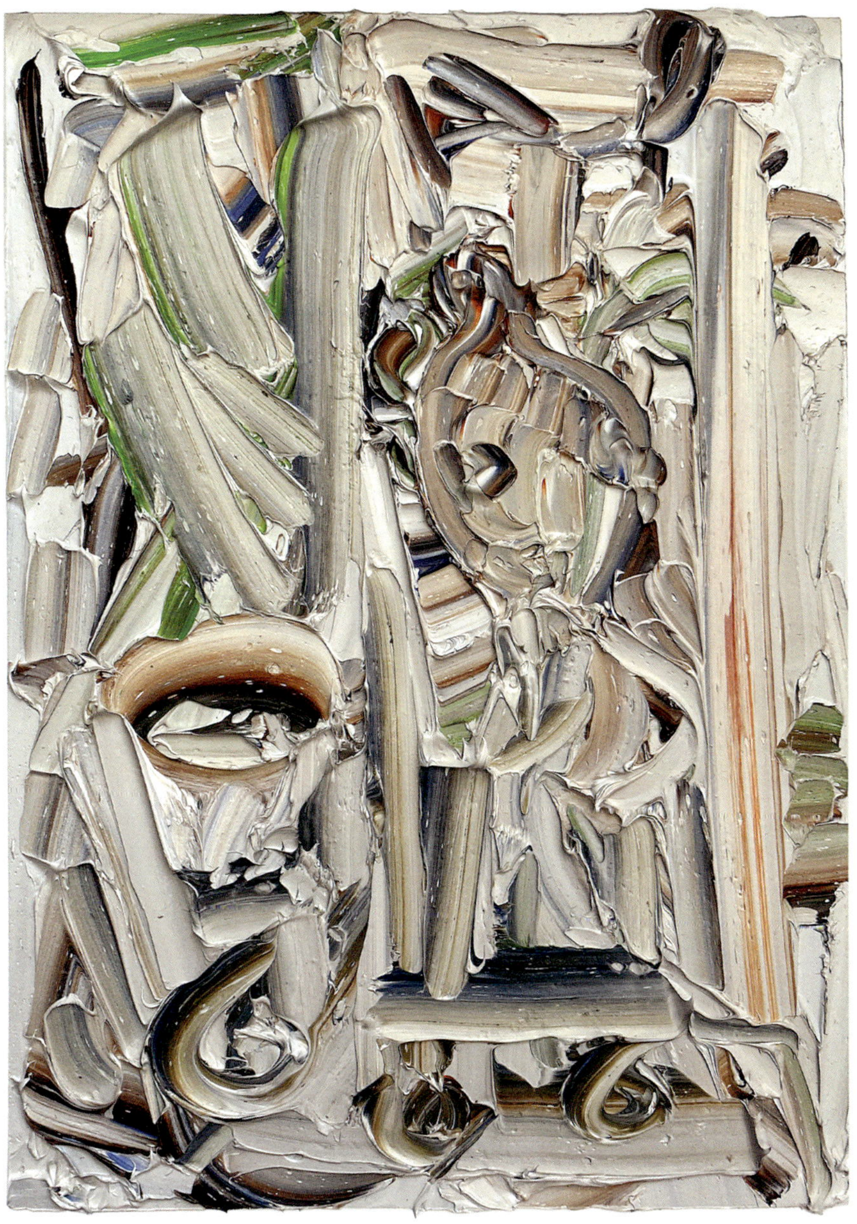

Waterfall, firefall, blue rush blaze,
Three graces, the sea gulls
Fly then land then lie peacefully
Together on sheets of reflected light.
There, on frozen rocks, they dream,
Recalling different days, the weather
Of different ethics and different rhymes,
Charm and beauty and creative mists
Becoming smoke for martyrs and anchorites,
Jazzmen and entranced ballerinas, all,
Now onto their ice, a white sheet on fire,
And in the sky above, the albatross,
Soaring and diving then sinking, in love.

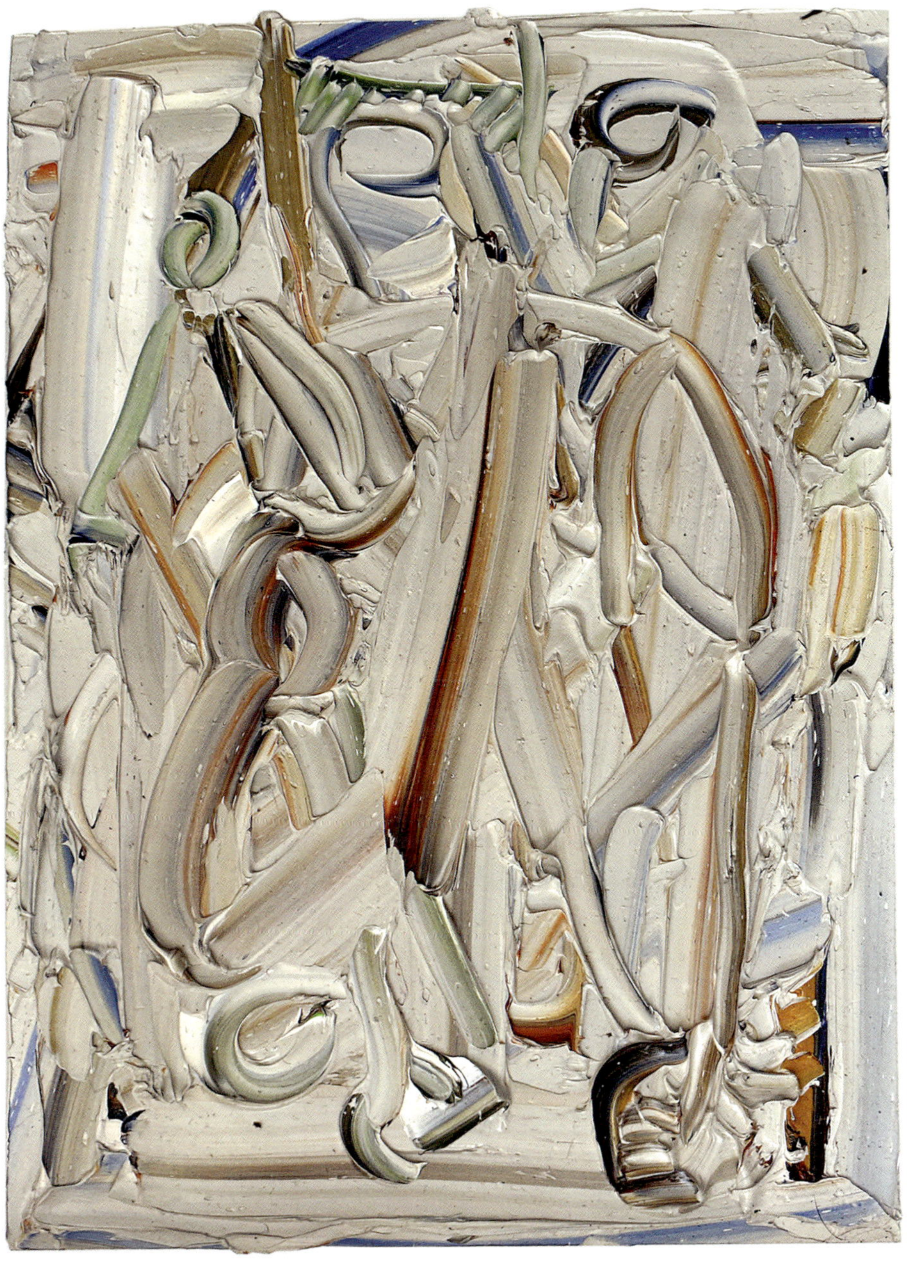

Ritz

The golden walk ends with a marble cake,
The best in the world, amber vanilla crumb,
Inset with a blossom of cocoa nib chocolate.
The lotus is traced with Matisse's old stylus,
And the old concierge brags about fulfilling,
Politely and with reserve, a request for elephant
Soup made from a refugee at the Paris Zoo.

Coco Chanel bedded Nazis upstairs, the lobby
A lapis lazuli encrusted road with gilded guiderails,
Memories of Manet seas tossed from blue rugs
Brought from the Shah's old palace in Tehran.
The best in the world, each display case
Radiates stitched cashmere and tweed,
And support staffs for canted civility.

And the golden walk, lined with diamonds,
Follows the tailored song of the martini,
A litany of cozy and blameless screams.

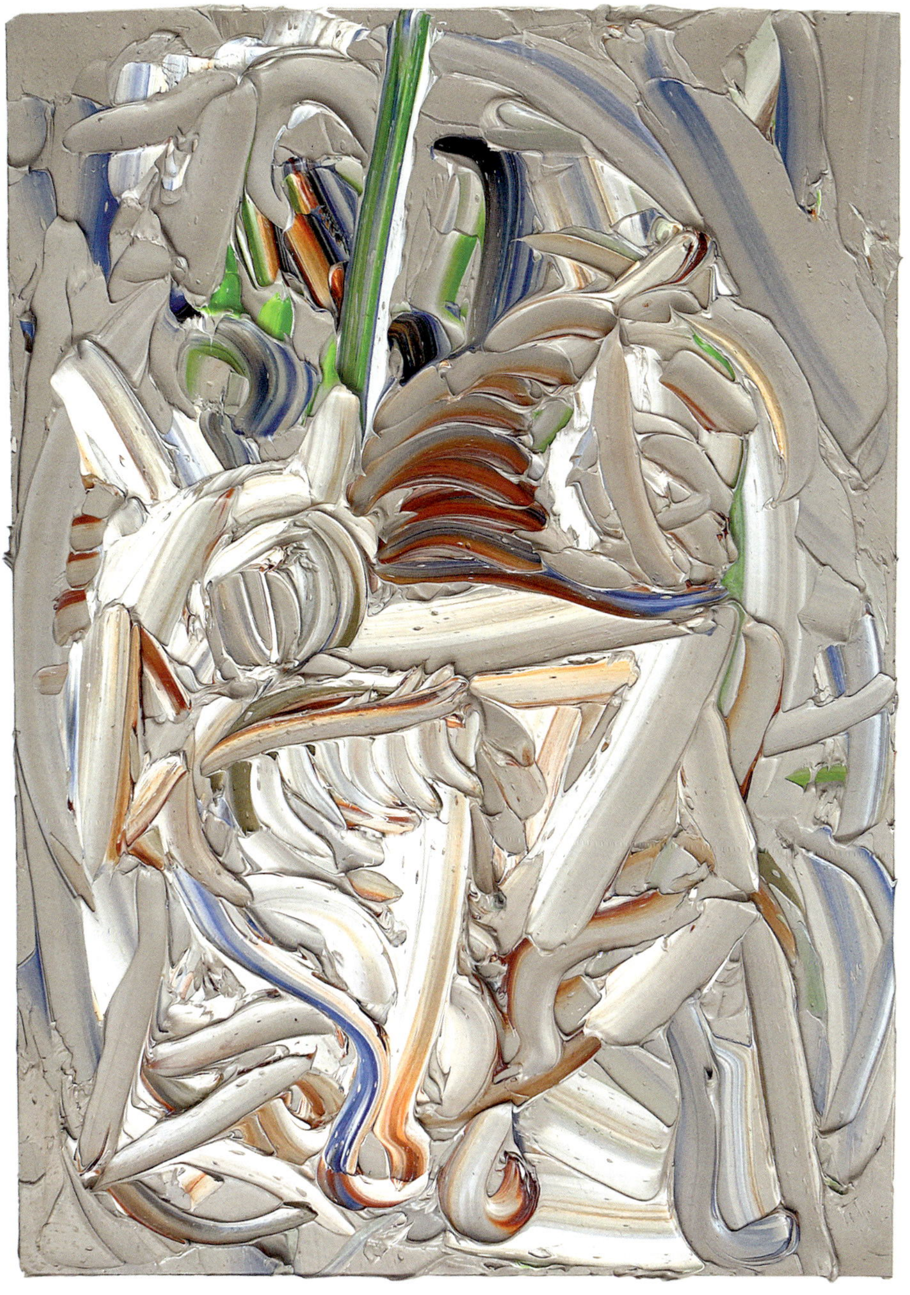

Hundred-degree summers without air conditioning,
Because my father's father would not have one,
And the old world must stubbornly judge the new.
And so our swamp cooler cycled through water,
Churning through what I would fill with a hose,
Shocked each time against its conductive metal,
Never grounded and always electric to the touch.

Inside, we played the movie Explorers with River Phoenix
So many times the VHS tape would skew off
Its wheel and distort the image on the screen.
We could see in the fuzz, boys working in a junkpile,
Gathering discarded wreckage and old transistors,
Creating a bubble in which they could float, launching
Themselves up outside into the wide clear sky.

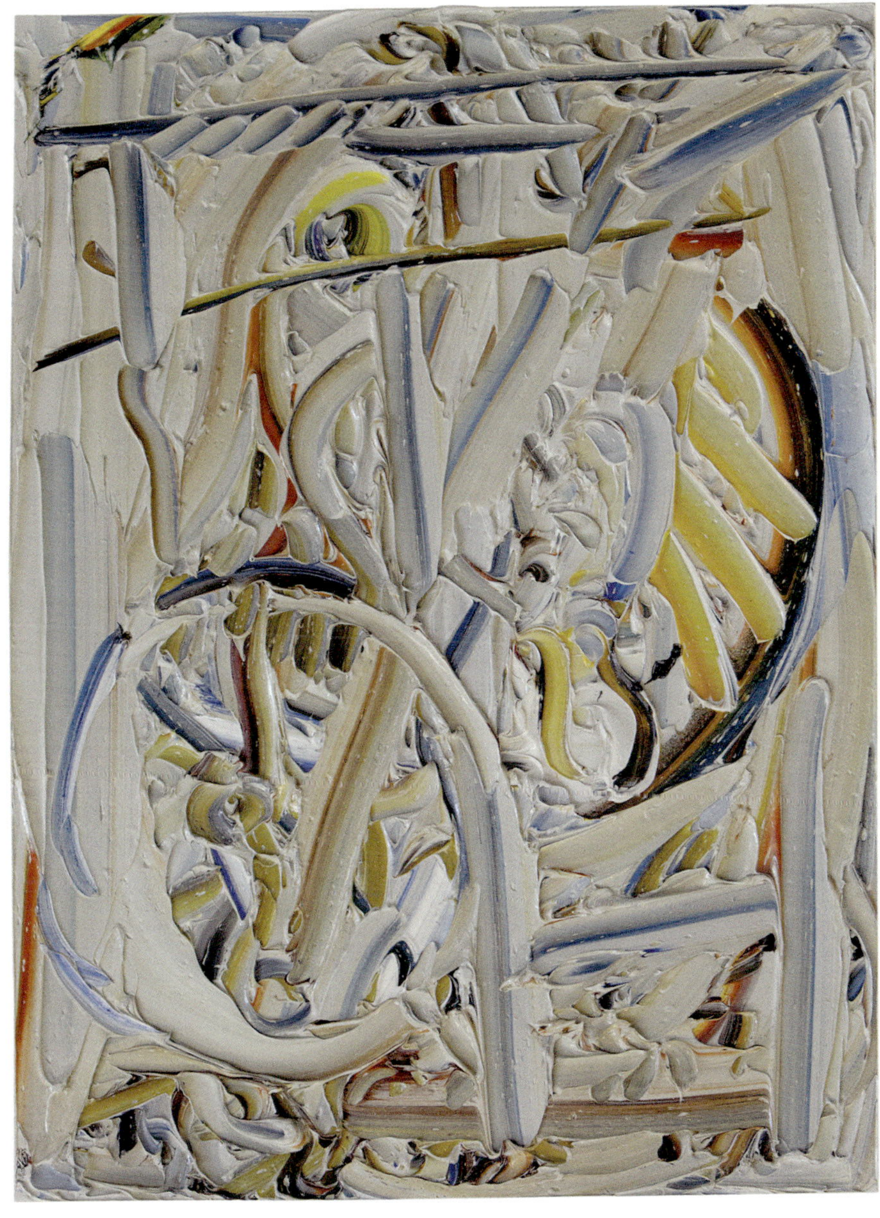

Always a panic, always unprepared and late,
You grab a chair and ram it under the doorknob.
Then the largest item in the room, a desk
Is pushed up, a shelf is turned over and placed.
After a breath, a series of firm knocks occurs:
Small tables, packing trunks, chests of drawers,
Folding screens, even tall lamps are stacked.

When the pounding starts, you look for anything —
Clothes, rugs, papers, teddy bears,
Guitars, poetry, paintings, knives, swords —
All to go against the door, pressed to its frame.
The hinges start to bend and the nails squeal:
Pounding now, tremors through it all, screaming
Metal numbly through it all, the dull hit of a broad axe.

The strike of a snowball on a shy kid's skull, more
Pounding, piling, pounding, piling, till it is all open,
And what must come through comes through, to arrival.

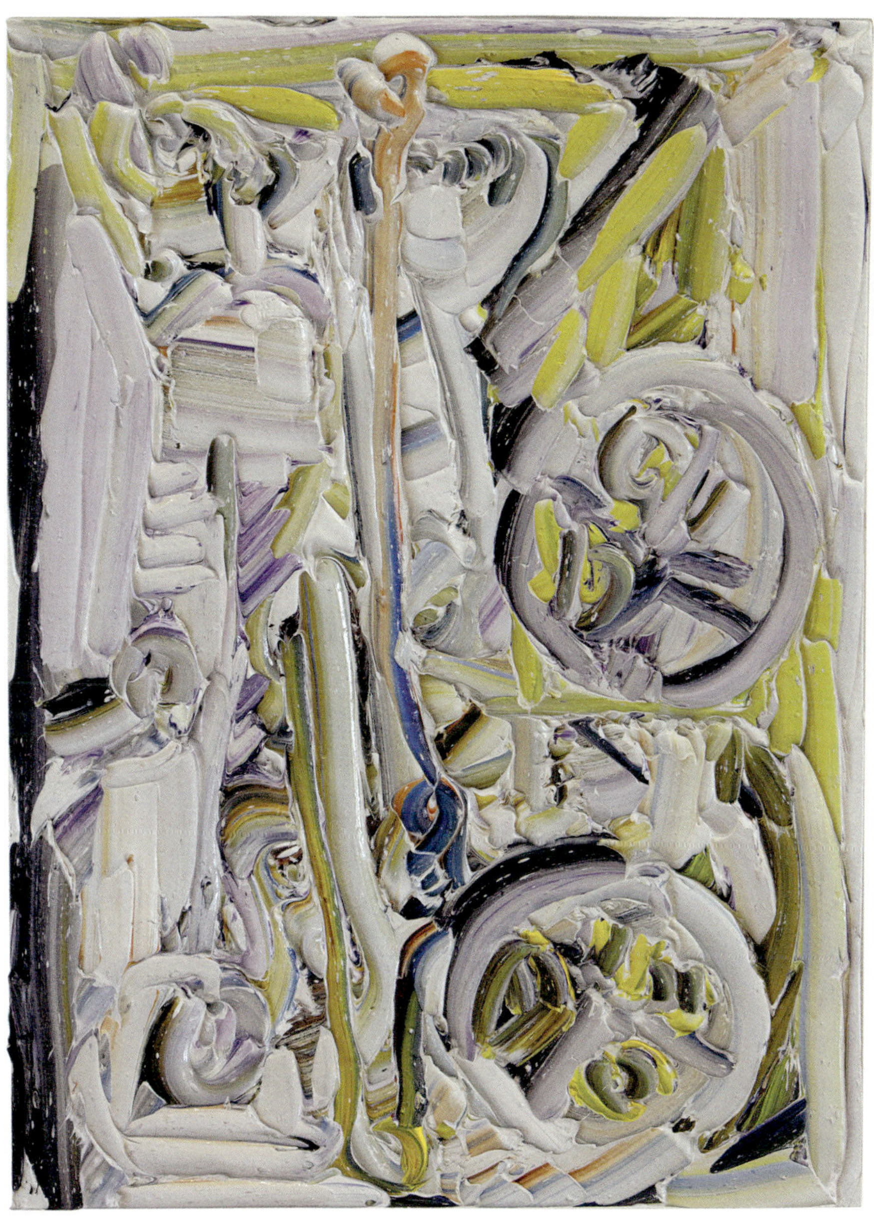

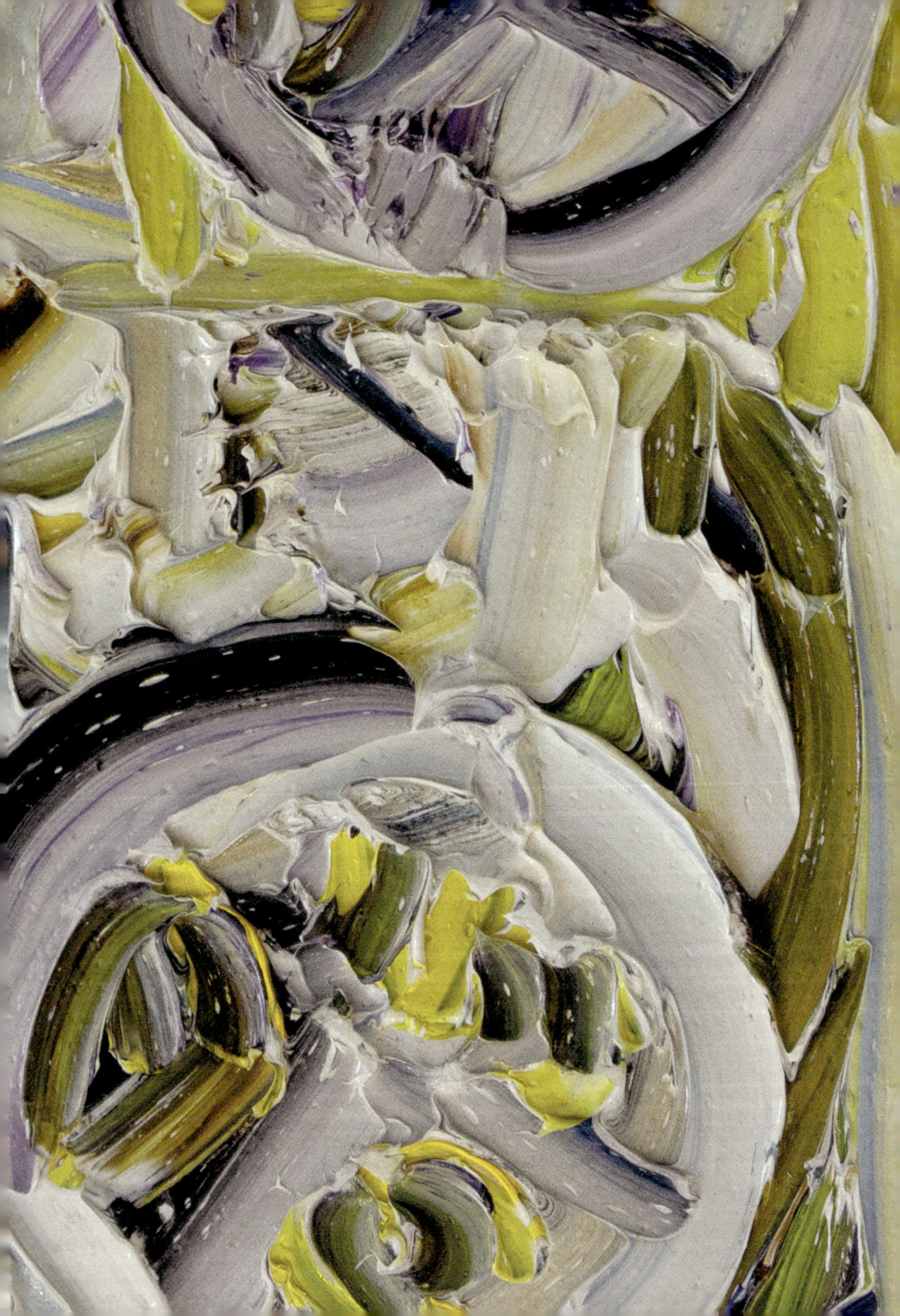

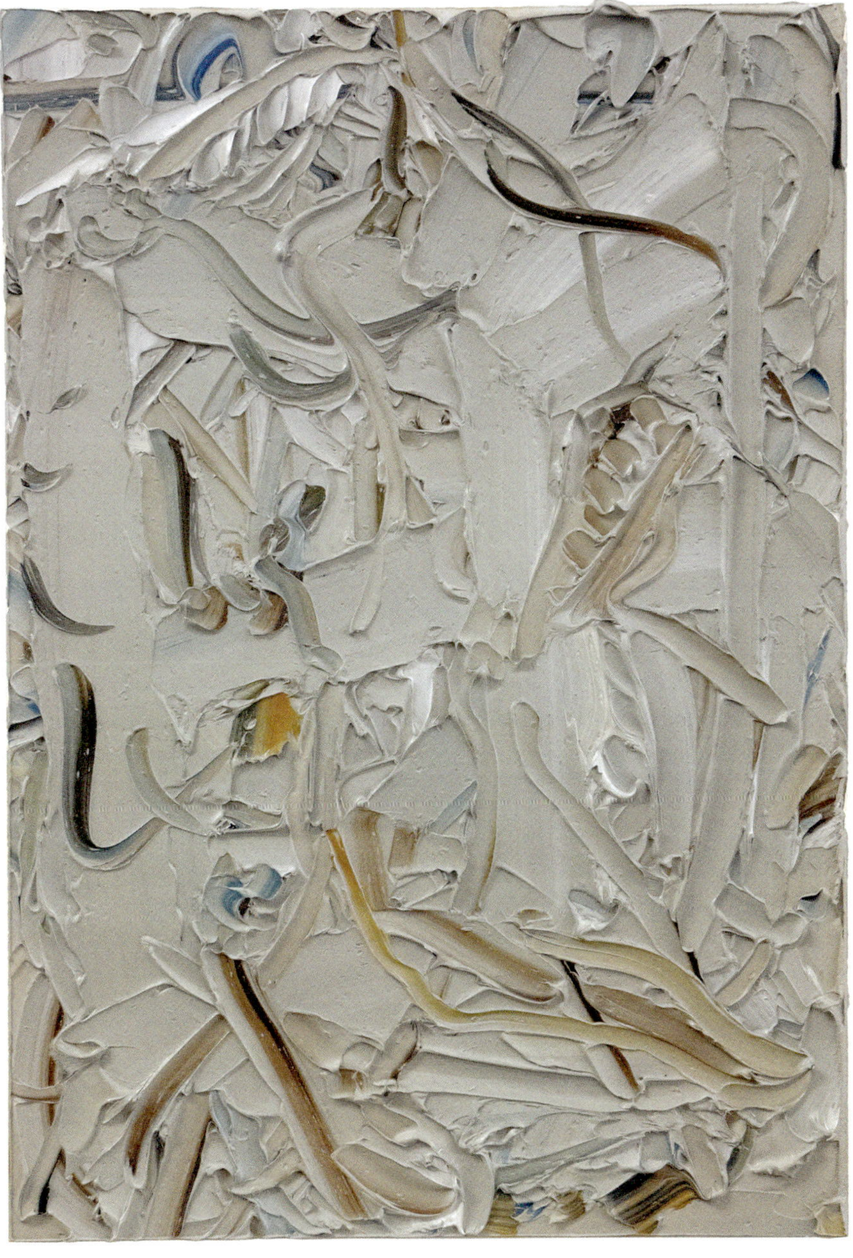

All the churning pumps below,
Pulling and driving and diving
Beneath our concrete crust,
Down track their pulse, forward,
No pockets in the line, up pump
And engine for time, honey pump
Glory pump breathing clocks.
Pump pump goes a man in anger
Who lost his pump pumping
Iron into milk. And the Frigate Bird,
Out on the rocks, pumps out
His red balloon pump, to multiply
The pumps in the water, the air,
The pipes, the pipes are pumping,
Answering threats from above.

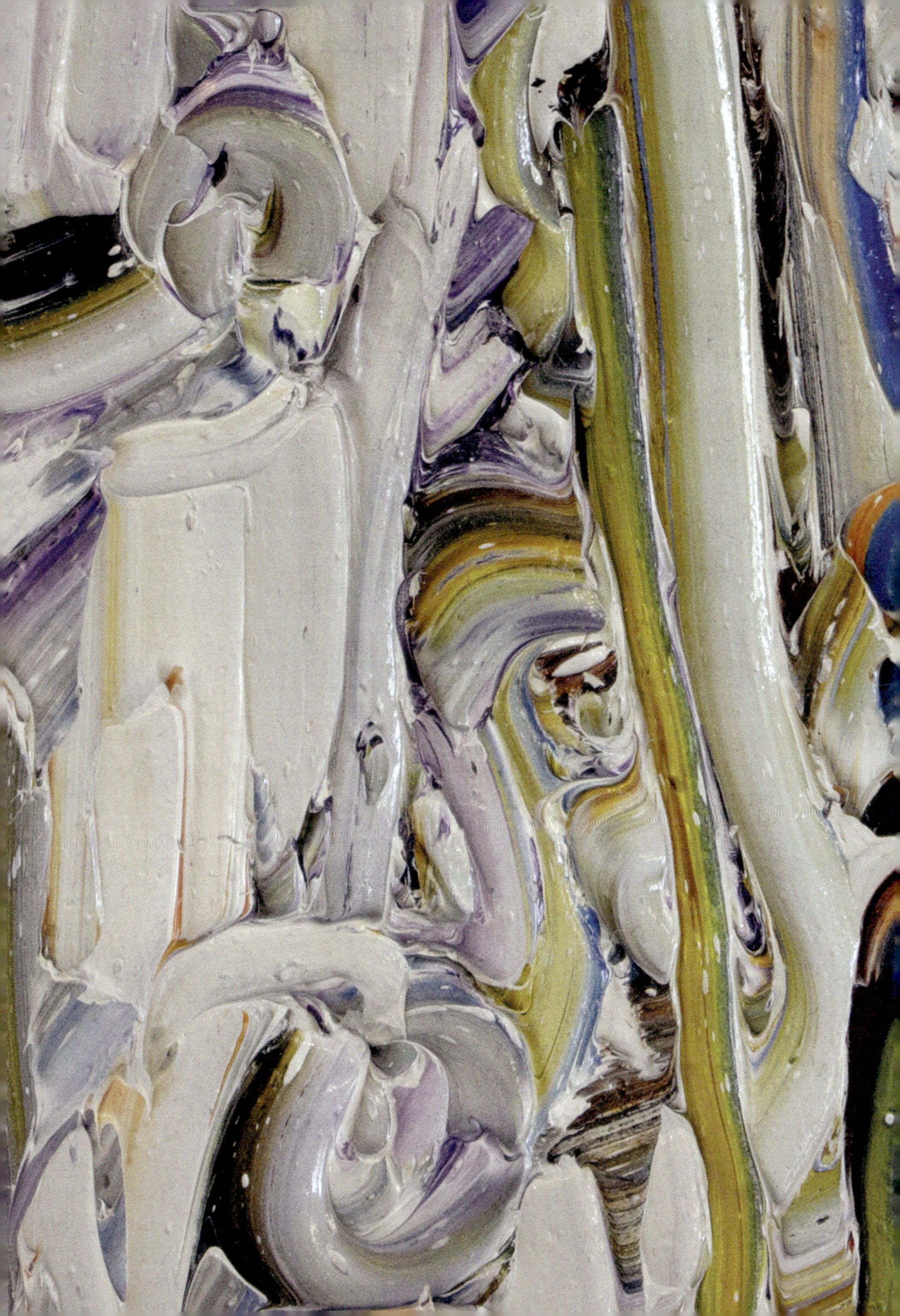

The banyan fingers down its hem
At the park on Collins in Miami,
Riotous gingers, birds of paradise
Cleave to hotels open in the heat.

A lush parade of hot skin dances
A dripping orgy of sweat and beat,
Sugar enough for eons of earth,
All over the red limit of plenty.

But there is a blue geyser of cloud,
A wind of upturned cold,
Far away from this tropic strip,
Slowly plunging into the sea.

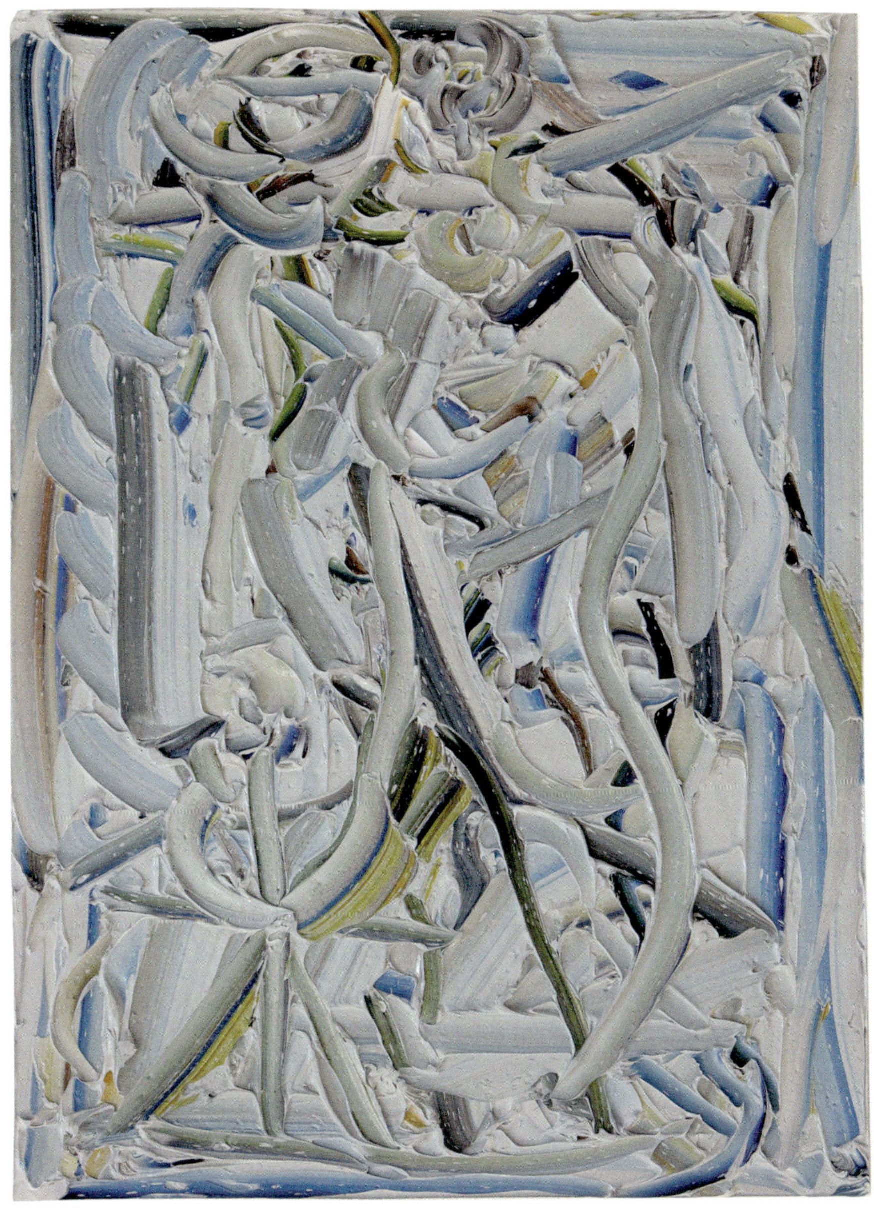

Wind and fog and rain
Drip sand solace, curtained
Sunlight's close collision
Of particle and pale rhythm
Rigging through the lung
Song of the misty day,
All in a painting by Whistler
Hung in a papered room
Full of pampered princes.

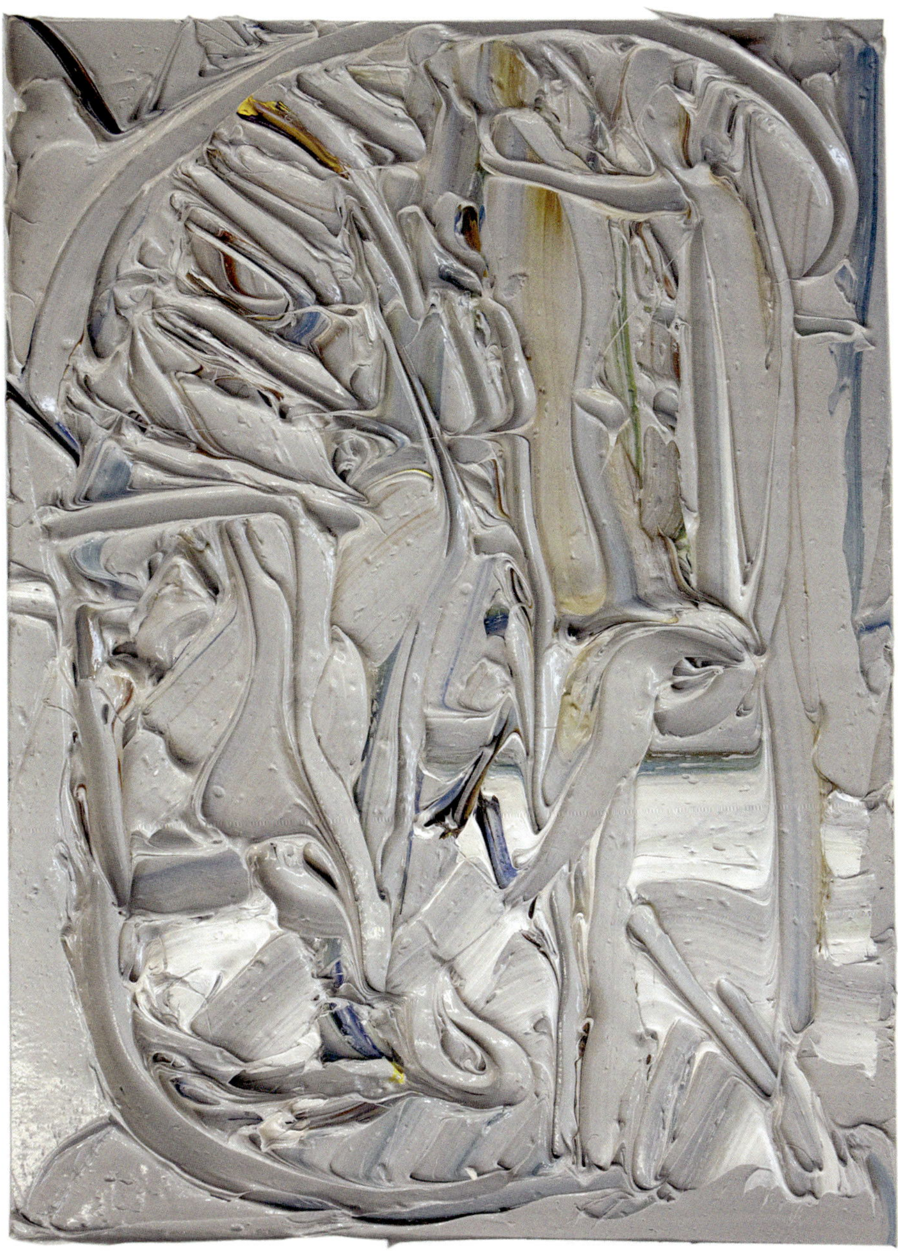

This is what I lost:

The working mystery
        Of how the land
        Slowly enters the body.
Candy boxes
        (Twix especially)
        In the freezer.
Stainless steel cereal bowls
        Sweating with milk.
Open claws, arching back
        But unable to pinch
        A well-placed hand
        On a crawdad's abdomen.
Meadowlark leaps and bowtie
        Flourishes of the scissortail
        Out in a limitless field.

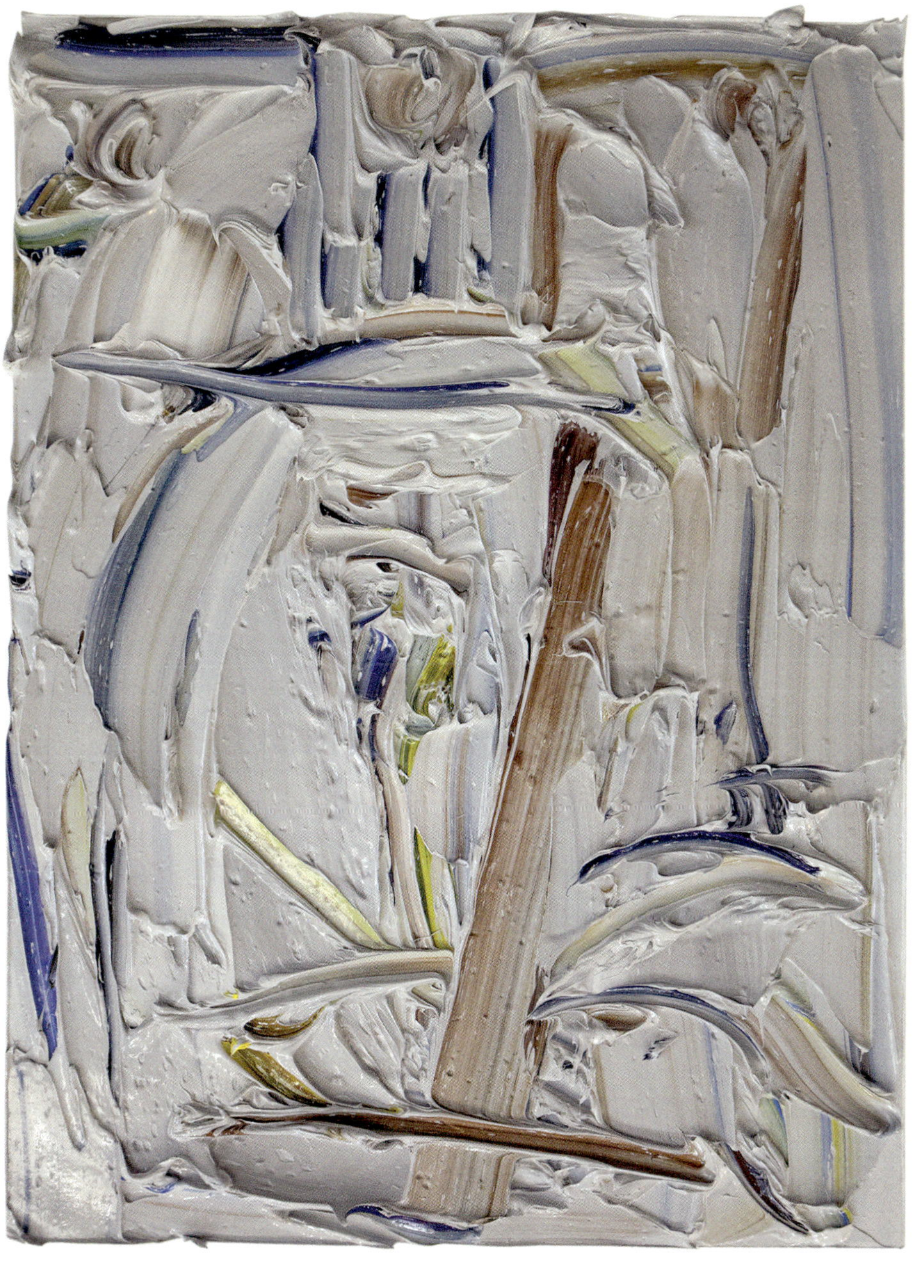

Omens

The morning birds — doves, sparrows, and domesticated parrots — give way to a tufted pair. They have rouge dabbed under their black eyes, rouge echoed in a patch between their white breasts and long grey tails tipped with white. From the tropics, they settled here among the also exiled palm trees. Extermination efforts failed. They had made it through, and they now nest in gardens away from guns and traps and poison. They are on my lawn, can be seen from my porch. Red Whiskered Bulbuls.

*

I find it increasingly hard to move. I question whether I want to move. I feel the equation sharply: engaging the physical world compounds risk. Movement brings little monsters which amplify the shadows and carry truths previously just out of view. I see them in the bushes, looking down from the trees, even present as daemons on the faces of friends or strangers in the street. These monsters are alive, threatening paralysis, threatening infection. Each thrust into the world is a thrust into them.

*

Others saw them too. They came for my family. They stared in from the edges of my childhood farm. They were vivid there, attacking there, and I had to find them. I camped on dirt pads under open skies, with a lantern light set on picnic tables. Cicadas landed on my chair. I remembered seeing their shells as a child, stuck to the bark of trees, attached with tiny, powerful intricacy. To remove the bodies was to rip them open, and in ripping them open, I felt like I was playing and having fun. In the lantern light, one cicada set my way its marbled head and dark eyes, eyes one with the darkness, from which a wind was blowing in.

*

And the wind would carry me, carry on, all the way into my childhood bedroom. The gusts struck against my farmhouse, lashing the windows. Unable to sleep, I tried to read the turbulence away and my reading light disrupted the flight patterns of bugs, who I now noticed with me in the same wind. They would hit the window and die. Reaching for the curtains and the switch, I found a frog suctioned onto the glass, his bubbled toes and his pink belly. He was asleep, unmoved, warmed, even comforted by the glow.

*

There were more snakes than usual. Under the stars, a green garter lay then sprung from the sidewalk in a quick, undulating line. Cottonmouths surfaced to break the smooth surface of the pond. A rat snake skittered off gravel into the tall dusty grass. A King. Another King. I began to believe the snakes could appear at any moment. My walking slowed, my eyes no longer on the sky but across the ground, rooting around in leaves and woodpiles, searching for that which was to appear. Tubes and hoses and spirals and coils. Undersides of rocks, holes next to ponds, under cars, behind the kitchen stove. Everywhere. Twisting and moving.

*

There was a fire in a trailer nearby. A neighbor who I had never met had stuffed it with a pack rat's treasure. The junk outgrew the trailer, outgrew the lot, and took to the fields in the forms of outmoded farm equipment and overbrimming rusting trucks. The projected future of the salvage man's ethic. The fire cleared these purposes, brought the entire enterprise to a halt. The fire extended into the neighbor's spirit. He took to cleaning and clearing, the fire's sudden pupil scouring the land. He carted the refuse off in massive scoops of a tractor loader. In patches of pressed grass where the trash had lain, a skunk was in panic in the 107-degree heat. She was far from crepuscular shadow, all black fur absorbing that furious sun, searching in the void for the nest, for the kit taken in the outcome of the blaze.

*

I never saw deer on the farm as a child. Their scarcity made me look actively for them when I went a few miles in any direction. Off to the north, they were present to the point of saturation, but since they were not on the farm, they were a perpetual novelty. The constant surprise of their arrival, as though a secret part of me had washed the decks of my mind of all previous encounters, brought a kinship, a partial understanding between me and those lovely, lithe creatures. We were bound together in that we both forgot each other immediately. In 2020, on the threshold of a thunderstorm, a deer finally wandered in, locked eyes with me and scampered off.

*

A single opened gate redrew the map. The cattle, having built up their patterns inside of their fields over months, saw their own paths again for the first time, as though they had never been in those fields. Their soft confusion was accompanied by new sources of food. A gate was left open, and in the dark, the cows wandered into new grass. A single calf was left behind. Calling to its mother, the call was returned, full of a need unexplained and unsatisfied by words like longing and love.

*

The road back was white stripes and hot skies, pandemic clouds and history's pain, bridges dedicated to Vietnam battles on land quieted by genocide. Everywhere the country's open, chewing mouth. The difference between a gulley and a ravine and canyon and a mesa. The strata and the petroglyph. I let the vista draw near, then go out so far and so fast. My eyes could not follow it. A raven lands, flies up and out into a sky that is all wing.

*

I collect all the images I have of a coyote and form a collage of him in my mind. I gather the image of him on the farm. I gather the image of him on the road, and I gather the image of him in the city. These join hundreds of other images, all perfect in and of themselves, now entering the mess of my mind. The coyote always lives and expresses perfectly the frame in which he is found. I find him in the field, a single vigilant creature set against the open. He is all that is, all that will be, a total vision, then gone. And on the road, he is running to the side. His is outside. He runs and I drive. I envy him, thinking that whatever knowledge may be does not seem to concern him, so he is integrated, so he is not separate in his movement from what moves. And on the porch, after the Bulbuls scatter, there is that brown coated, skinny survivor, pacing in the flicker of the streetlight. I find his droppings in the morning, all twisted up in dry string and regurgitated bone, grey and ready for a world of ash.

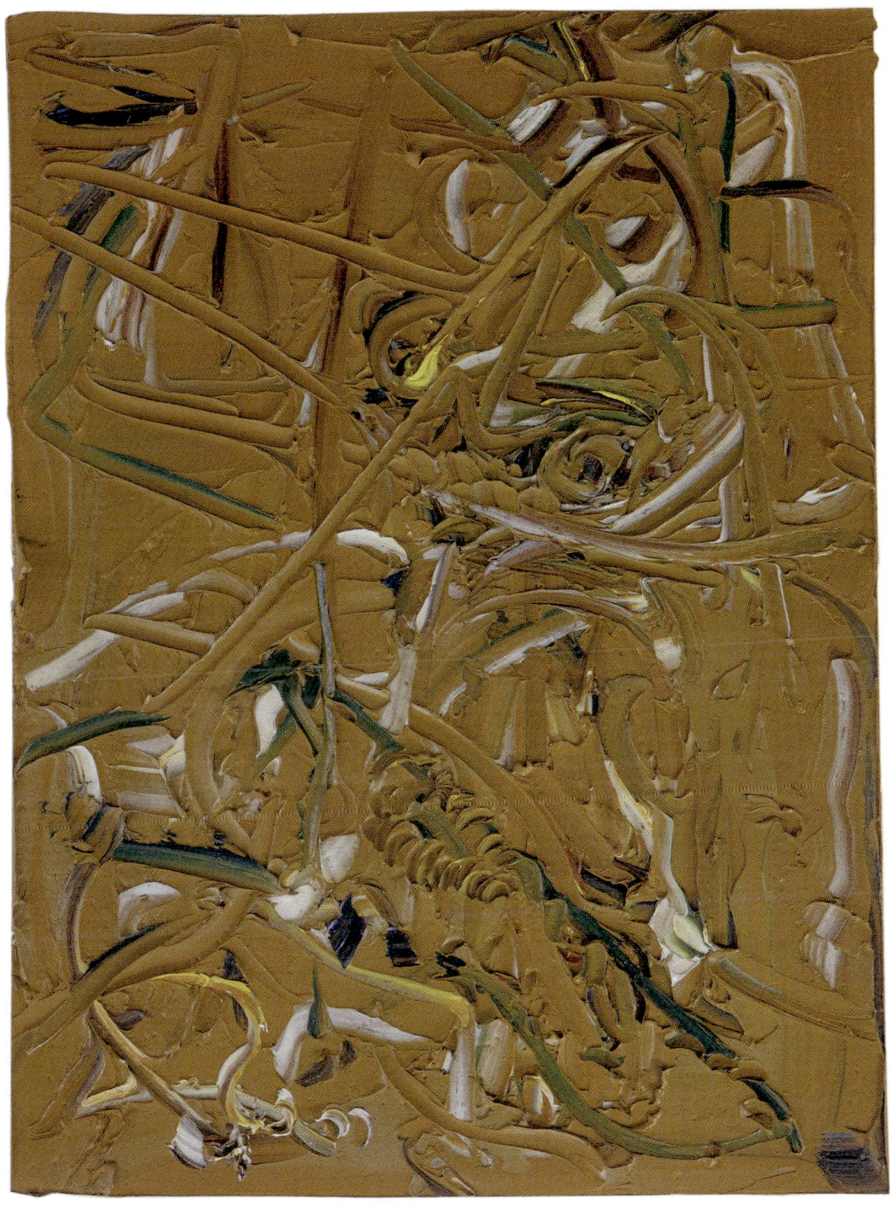

Cover
Eye and Circle, 2020 (detail)
oil on paper, 11 x 8 inches
Collection Turki Al Khater, Doha

7
Still Life, 2020
oil on paper, 11 x 8 inches

9
Yellow, 2020
oil on paper, 11 x 8 inches
Private collection, Sydney, Australia

11
The Stage, 2020
oil on paper, 11 x 8 inches
Collection Marla and Mitch

13
Letters I, 2020
oil on paper, 12 x 9 inches
Private collection, Sydney, Australia

15
The Boat, 2020
oil on paper, 9 1/4 x 12 1/4 inches

17
Soft, 2020
oil on paper, 12 1/4 x 8 1/4 inches

19
Face I, 2020
oil on paper, 12 x 9 inches

21
Letters III, 2020
oil on paper, 11 1/4 x 8 1/4 inches
Private collection, Sydney, Australia

22, 23
Letters III, 2020 (detail)
oil on paper, 11 1/4 x 8 1/4 inches
Private collection, Sydney, Australia

25
Flowers, 2020
oil on paper, 14 x 10 1/4 inches

27
Still Life II, 2020
oil on paper, 14 x 10 1/4 inches
Private collection, Germany

29
Night at the Sea, 2020
oil on linen, 12 1/4 x 18 1/4 inches

31
Red, 2020
oil on paper, 12 1/4 x 9 1/4 inches

33
Her Face, 2020
oil on paper, 14 1/4 x 10 1/4 inches

35
Emptied, 2020
oil on paper, 13 3/4 x 9 1/2 inches

37
Offering, 2020
oil on paper, 14 1/2 x 10 3/4 inches

39
Gray, 2020
oil on paper, 14 1/4 x 10 1/4 inches

41
Two Figures, 2020
oil on paper, 11 1/2 x 8 1/4 inches
Private collection, Sydney, Australia

43
Bird-Like, 2020
oil on paper, 11 x 8 inches
Collection Sami & Justin Grefé

45
Figure and Mouth, 2020
oil on paper, 11 x 8 inches
Private collection, Chicago

46, 47
Figure and Mouth, 2020 (detail)
oil on paper, 11 x 8 inches
Collection Sami & Justin Grefé

49
Letters VIII, 2020
oil on paper, 11 x 8 inches
Private collection, Santa Monica

51
Head, 2020
oil on paper, 11 x 8 inches
Private collection, South Haven, Michigan

53
The Group, 2020
oil on paper, 11 x 8 inches
Private collection, Sydney, Australia

55
Elongated Face, 2020
oil on paper, 12 x 8 inches
Collection Robyn Tavel, Chicago

57
Line, 2020
oil on paper, 11 1/4 x 8 1/4 inches

59
Eye and Circle, 2020
oil on paper, 11 x 8 inches
Collection Turki Al Khater, Doha

61
Split in Two, 2020
oil on paper, 11 x 8 inches
Courtesy PATRON Gallery, Chicago

63
Soldier, 2020
oil on paper, 11 x 8 inches
Private collection, Chicago

65
Violet, 2020
oil on paper, 11 x 8 inches
Private collection, Sydney, Australia

67
Night Walk, 2020
oil on paper, 11 1/4 x 9 3/4 inches
Private collection, New York

69
What Passes Doesn't Fall into a Void, 2021
oil on paper, 12 x 9 inches
Private collection, Sydney, Australia

71
Bottles, 2020
oil on paper, 11 1/4 x 8 1/4 inches

73
Figure and Earth IV, 2021
oil on paper, 12 by 9 inches
Private collection, Sydney, Australia

75
Figures, 2021
oil on paper, 8 x 10 inches
Private collection, Sydney, Australia

77
Circles, 2021
oil on paper, 8 x 10 inches
Private collection, Sydney, Australia

79
Grid, 2021
oil on paper, 12 x 9 inches

81
Wheels, 2021
oil on paper, 12 x 9 1/4 inches

82, 83
Wheels, 2021 (detail)
oil on paper, 12 x 9 1/4 inches

85
Blue, 2021
oil on paper, 12 x 9 1/4 inches

87
The Sea, 2022
oil on paper, 12 1/4 x 9 1/4 inches
Private collection, Germany

89
Face, 2022
oil on paper, 12 1/4 x 9 1/4 inches
Private collection, Germany

93
Omens, 2021
oil on paper, 12 x 9 inches
Veronica M. Fernandez, Mexico City

This book was created in conjunction with the exhibition:
Liat Yossifor
small seas
April 11 – May 11, 2023

Harris Gallery
University of La Verne
1950 Third Street
La Verne, CA 91750
www.laverne.edu

Liat Yossifor and Ed Schad would like to thank Dion Johnson and Carrie Paterson.

Ed Schad would like to thank Liat Yossifor, Heather Hart, his mom Elaine Schad, and his dad E.J. Schad, who introduced him to poetry and taught him that poetry can be a lifetime love.

Liat Yossifor would like to thank Ed Schad, Yfat Yossifor, Ross Berger, PATRON Gallery, Chicago, Fox Jensen Gallery, Australia, Veronica M. Fernandez, and Leora and Oded Yossifor.

Photography:
Yfat Yossifor and Jeff McLane, Los Angeles.

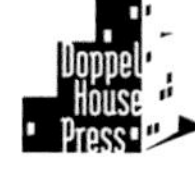

DoppelHouse Press | Los Angeles | doppelhouse.com

ISBN: 9781954600201
Library of Congress Control Number: 2023934404